S0-BPC-474

POWER
WITH
PURPOSE

JOHN SIMS

POWER
WITH
PURPOSE

The Holy Spirit in Historical
and
Contemporary Perspective

JOHN SIMS

POWER WITH PURPOSE

The Holy Spirit in Historical and Contemporary Perspective

PATHWAY
PRESS

ISBN:0-87148-716-0
Library of Congress No.: 84-61528

© Copyright 1984

Pathway Press
Cleveland, Tennessee

This Book is Affectionately
Dedicated to my Wife,
PATRICIA KAY
My Mother
THEO SIMS
And
The Memory of my Sister
FREDA

Contents

Preface

A preface may be an effort to supply the rationale for the writing of a book, or it may informally introduce the topic or philosophy of the contents. I would like to use this preface to briefly do both and, in addition, acknowledge those whose help and encouragement have made it possible.

In his Gifford Lectures, John Baillie told the parable of the degree candidate who sat staring at the questions placed before him by the examiner. Unable to write anything, the candidate replied that the questions were too difficult. "Well," replied the examiner, "put down what you know."

Theologians and Bible scholars generally agree that it is difficult to theologize about the Holy Spirit. He simply transcends our finite conceptions of Him and refuses to be domesticated by our theological systems. No subject is more tender or touches the secret and mysterious workings of God more profoundly than this one. No one should be pretentious enough to think that he has all the answers about the Holy Spirit. After writing a massive work on the subject, Abraham Kuyper confessed, "The need for divine guidance is never more deeply felt than when one undertakes to give instruction about the Holy Spirit."

Like the hesitant candidate, I too feel that many questions about the Holy Spirit are difficult to answer. But I also believe that it is time to write down some things that I believe and know about the Holy Spirit. There are important issues that the Pentecostal needs to face and address at this point in his history. The opportunity for me to begin this personal project came in 1981/82 when then President Charles W. Conn and the Lee College Board of Directors granted me a sabbatical leave so that I could accept a Visiting Fellowship at Princeton Theological Seminary. I am grateful both to Lee College and to Princeton Theological Seminary for making the initial work of this book possible. I give special thanks to colleagues and friends at both institutions and especially to President Conn who contributed significantly through his support of a sabbatical leave program at Lee College.

This book is written from a Pentecostal perspective, and I have attempted throughout to bear witness to a faith that I believe has meaning, power, and relevance for today. The material has been organized around key issues and doctrines with which, I am convinced, Pentecostals must presently deal. One of the objectives has been to provide some historical perspective from which Pentecostal theology can be identified and articulated—particularly in relation to the Roman Catholic and mainline Protestant traditions and their understanding of the Holy Spirit. The thesis that binds the various strands of the book together is the conviction that the power of the Holy Spirit is "power with purpose."

I trust that this work on the Holy Spirit will serve the needs of the general lay reader and the student in the classroom. It is difficult to write a book that will do both, but I have had both sets of readers in mind throughout. It is a book that I feel can be most profitable if it is studied as well as read. I am particularly pleased that it will be studied in the Church of God Bible Institute Program.

Special acknowledgement is due Dr. French L. Arrington who read the manuscript in its initial stage and offered many helpful suggestions. Dr. Robert E. Fisher, Dr. James D. Jenkins, the Reverend Hoyt E. Stone, the Reverend Robert D. McCall, and the staff of the Department of General Education have played a vital role in preparing this book for publication. My special thanks to them. I cannot forget my lovely wife Pat who has offered valuable advice and encouragement, or my three sons, John Patrick, Matthew, and Mark whose patient curiosity about the book can now be satisfied. I give my special love and gratitude to those who taught and nurtured me in the Pentecostal faith, especially my mother and grandmother on whose farm the Church of God was first established in our county.

John Sims
Lee College
June 1984

Foreword

To say that I am pleased and in accord with this study of the Holy Spirit by John A. Sims would be a gross understatement. I am delighted, even enthusiastic, about it; reading the manuscript has given me mental stimulation and spiritual enrichment.

But then, I have long been impressed and blessed by the works of Dr. Sims. As a theological scholar he has always revealed clarity of thought and sincerity in his approach to the Word of God. As a teacher he demonstrates sensitivity and persuasiveness in the presentation of doctrine. And now as a writer he carries those strengths a step further by writing with lucid power in a difficult field.

Satisfactory studies of the Holy Spirit have always been hard to come by. Perhaps one reason for this is man's inability to see the Spirit as He is, to truly comprehend His position in the divine Godhead. Until recent years there were only a handful of worthy works in the complex field of pneumatology. For the greater part, these were time-worn standards in theological literature. In more recent times, especially with the rise of the Pentecostal movement and the Charismatic renewal, a great deal of interest has been kindled in the Holy Spirit. There is a growing concern about the Spirit's place in the works of God and the affairs of man.

Unfortunately, much of the current literature has been flawed by immature understanding and extravagant treatment. Too often the subject has suffered at the hands of those with a Corinthian-like leaning toward the sensational or the controversial. This circumstance makes all the more welcome such a sound and balanced work as this one.

Dr. Sims has utilized the finest research methods in his study. He has supported his work with classic pneumatalogical statements by earlier and contemporary theologians, but the strength of the book is in his own insights and reasoned truth. The book therefore has a heart, a heart given it by the writer from his own experience and from the Word of God.

And now, if the favorable circumstances of attention and distribution will only smile upon the book, and I pray that they will, it may well become the standard, even the classic, resource on the Holy Spirit in our generation. It is a worthy candidate for such a happy possibility.

—Charles W. Conn

Chapter 1

Power for Purposeful Living

The Need for Power With Purpose

The doctrine of the Holy Spirit is one of Christianity's most severely abused doctrines. From the earliest period of church history until the Protestant Reformation the pendulum of abuse swung from those who attempted to restrict the freedom of the Spirit to fixed patterns of church order and authority to those free-spirited radicals of whom Martin Luther said scornfully: "They pretend to have swallowed the Holy Ghost [symbolized by the dove], feathers and all!"

The extremism and abuse that earlier accompanied the doctrine of the Holy Spirit has been just as evident in modern times. The twentieth century has witnessed the emergence of Pentecostal churches and a charismatic movement within the historic denominations, but with them have come some ambiguity and unbalanced views about God as Spirit. Among some, discussions about the Holy Spirit focus upon the Christian's experience of the Holy Spirit. Personal and emotional effects of the Spirit are stressed, but little attention is given to the purpose for such experiences or to aspects of the Spirit's person and work that do not relate to human experience. Among others, there is a strong theology of the Holy Spirit but little evidence of spiritual empowerment. There is plenty of light and understanding, but the power of the Spirit is absent.

Power without Purpose is No power at all. UN-HARNESSED POWER

Increasing numbers of Christians today are unwilling to separate power and purpose. They recognize that the need is for Spirit-empowered men and women who are willing to become instruments of the divine purpose. There is no viable alternative to a theology of the Holy Spirit. The only alternative to a well-thought-out theology that takes full account of the Spirit's person and work is a hodgepodge theology of unexamined concepts and feelings. More and more Pentecostals and charismatics are now seeking to understand the purpose of the Spirit's power. They realize that power in the absence of purpose can be chaotic, even destructive, while purpose without power is impotent. Just as a pair of scissors cannot function properly without both blades, the church cannot be what is was intended to be without both power and purpose.

A SYMBIOTIC RELATIONSHIP

The word "symbiosis" is a biological term. It refers to things which are functionally distinct but have an inseparable relationship. Power and purpose have such a relationship. They are not the same; one can exist without the other. But like an organism that must have all of its parts functioning properly, the church must have both power and purpose if it is to be a true Pentecostal church. The Church of the living God is a living organism. It functions properly only when there is an operative and inseparable relationship between these two.

The Holy Spirit released in our lives is the spiritual parallel to the smashed atom in nature. The atom must be smashed before its energy can be released and utilized. God's power must be operative in us before we can become what God intends. But power alone is not enough. It must be purposefully channeled. Atomic power can light a city or it can destroy it. It all depends upon the way the power is used. The great need in the church today is for a better understanding of spiritual power and how God wills to use it.

DISCOVERING GOD'S PURPOSE IN THE CREATED ORDER

It is exciting to experience the power of the Holy Spirit in our lives. Through the Holy Spirit God makes His steadfast love real to us. He allows us to experience the power of the future, to have a foretaste of the power of the Age to Come. There should not be any doubt that the Holy Spirit of Scripture is a personal power and presence that can be experienced. But neither should there be any doubt that God is also at work in the processes of nature and history. A Christian doctrine of the Holy Spirit recognizes that the work of the Holy Spirit is broader in scope than the realm of human experience. His power and presence find expression in the working out of a comprehensive purpose. God is real in the natural and historical process just as He is in the transforming moment. Much of our experience of the Holy Spirit is the experience of a particular moment, of a spiritual breakthrough, but it is also exciting to discover God's purpose in the created order. Discovering the eternal within the realm of the temporal and the mundane can broaden our understanding of God's activity in the world.

In his book, *The Traces of God,* Diogenes Allen asks us to imagine two intersecting planes which may help us to conceive of God as a reality who is beyond us but who also reaches us at that point where the divine plane crosses the human. At the intersection of the two planes, God makes Himself knowable and available through the Holy Spirit. Where the divine plane crosses the human plane in creation, through divine activity in history, or through our personal experience of Him, we come into contact with divine reality. It is through this revelatory contact that we are able to acknowledge the working of a spiritual purpose.

"If we become open to the presence of another reality in, but not of the world," Allen says, "we shall begin to find that He crosses our plane in many places. In time, we can even come to realize that not only does He touch us here and there, but that the entire human plane is in contact with the divine reality in which we live and move and have our being."[1]

A Pentecostal understanding of the Holy Spirit ought not to be one that dichotomizes the God who reveals Himself in religious experience from the God who is the Creator and sovereign Governor of history. The political scientist needs to understand that it is God's sovereignty over history that determines the rise and fall of nations, the medical doctor that it is God who "knows our frame" and "heals our diseases," the psychologist that He alone "knows all our thoughts," the astronomer that He "calls the stars by name," and the farmer that God is the source of the earth's increase. There can be no ultimate contradiction between the truth revealed in Scripture and truth as it is discovered in the arts and sciences. When Christians embrace the fact that God is the Author of all fact and reality they can joyfully affirm the words from the hymn "This is my Father's World." They can study the sciences and enjoy wholesome art forms, knowing that the more they know about truth, goodness, and beauty, the more they will know about the One who is their source. "Whatever anyone has said that is true," Justin Martyr said, "belongs to us, the Christians."

THE DANGER OF OVER-SPIRITUALIZING THE HOLY SPIRIT

As strange as it may seem, there is a danger of over-spiritualizing the work of the Holy Spirit. The danger is real because of the fateful tendency of some to separate spirit and nature, to set the physical and the material against the spiritual. This tendency can be traced historically through Platonism, ancient Gnosticism, Montanism, various forms of mysticism, the "inner light" doctrine of the Quakers, and other spiritual movements. Unfortunately, many still find this way of thinking attractive. Scripture clearly teaches, however, that a spirit/nature dualism is wrong. Nature is one of the realms in which the Holy Spirit works to accomplish God's purpose. The Holy Spirit is at work in the world, in matter, just as He is in the individual's heart. A spirit/nature dualism errs because it divorces one from the realities of earthly existence. It results in an erroneous understanding of who we are and how we are to minister.

Jesus saw people as whole people. He did not separate physical needs from spiritual needs. Jesus offered wholeness of body, mind, and spirit as well as holiness of heart. When Christians see people only in terms of spirits and souls they see less than Jesus saw, and they will inevitably offer less than Jesus offered. If we are to minister as Jesus ministered we must not allow the Holy Spirit to be removed from the physical realities of life, either in our thinking or our actions.

Marxist communism is one of the great tragedies of the twentieth century. But Christians must bear part of the blame because they abandoned man's physical and material needs and turned the poor and the oppressed over to secular agencies. The promise to speak more relevantly and compassionately to poverty and oppression has made Marxism plausible to millions. Karl Marx, the father of modern communism, was a materialist. Materialism holds that matter is the ultimate stuff of reality. It rejects all moral and spiritual realities beyond man himself and thus attempts to live by "bread alone." The heresy of Marx did not lie in his concern for man's material needs but in his underlying philosophy of materialism. For while Christianity acknowledges man's need for bread and material necessities, it also teaches that man has a more basic need. The threat of meaninglessness, of being irrevocably "lost," of missing the mark in life is even worse than being poor and hungry. But then again, Christians need not opt for an either/or. As ministers of Jesus Christ, Christians are called to minister to people as whole persons. "Inasmuch as ye have done it unto one of these my brethren," Jesus said, "ye have done it unto me."

THE ERROR OF NATURALISM

Christianity teaches that nature is a part of what we are; naturalism teaches that it is all that we are. Naturalists have concluded with Bertrand Russell that it is practically "beyond dispute" that the world as presented by modern science is quite purposeless, void of meaning, "the outcome of accidental collocations of atoms," justifying in man nothing but the grim mood of "unyielding despair." But if we understand life only in terms of natural forces, then we must be prepared to understand ourselves as a mere product of the uncertainties of time and chance. Man is merely the grand prize winner in the evolutionary sweepstakes. All of life stands under the threat of decay and death, and we conclude with Shakespeare's Macbeth that life is nothing more than "a tale told by an idiot, full of sound and fury, signifying nothing."

Pitirim Sorokin, an eminent sociologist, characterized the culture of our time as Sensate. A Sensate culture is one in which all reality has been reduced to the physical and material. Reality is what we know through the senses. Morality is largely a matter of style. Moral conduct is geared to promote human happiness, comfort, and pleasure here on earth for this is, from the naturalist point of view, the only world we will ever know. Psychologically, this view of man reduces him to a mechanistic animal, a mere combination of conditional and unconditional reflexes. Economically, there is a greater concentration on wealth-for-the-sake-of-wealth. Man is motivated more by his stomach than his ideals. Art forms reflect man's lustful quest for sensual reality. Since Sensate ethics are nothing more than man-made rules, they can be changed anytime one likes. Everything is relative.

In a Sensate society spiritual values do not exist, contracts and covenants lose their binding power, force and fraud are required to maintain moral order, governments become more unstable and more inclined to resort to violence, families disintegrate, "gimmicks" replace genius, the marketplace is glutted with sensually appealing materials, levels of living grow worse and life in general becomes less secure. Sorokin's descriptions of our day are pessimistic, but they accurately portray the conditions in our Sensate culture. It is a long way from the Apostle Paul to Hugh Hefner, the infamous owner of

Playboy magazine who epitomizes a Sensate culture. But it was a path man was doomed to travel once he forsook the realm of absolute values and ideals. When there are no more spiritual values by which to live and die, man is fated to live by sensual reality alone. The church is not immune from the influences of a Sensate culture. It must constantly guard against being put into the mold of worldly views and values. Christians must know who they are and the purpose for which they were created.

Christians affirm the Creator Spirit and the created order because creation tells us who we are, not because it is all that we are. God created the world and man, and He sustains them moment by moment. Man is part of nature, but he is more than nature. Man was created in God's own image so that he could have fellowship with God through the Holy Spirit. Man's moral and spiritual endowments anticipate more than an animal existence. He was created by God and for God. This world can never satisfy desires that have their source in another world. Man instinctively aspires to a life and destiny that is appropriate for one who is a child of God.

DISCOVERING GOD'S PURPOSE IN HISTORY AND HUMAN RELATIONSHIPS

The idea of history as a purposeful process was foreign to man's thinking in the ancient world. The succession of the seasons, the ceaseless return of night and day, and the movements of the heavenly bodies seemed to be self-evident signs that time was not going anywhere except in a circle. There seemed to be no meaningful end toward which things moved. Life was filled with melancholy and despair until the Hebrew Christian faith offered an explanation of history that gave meaning to the triumphs and tragedies of life. The underlying conviction of the faith was that God is guiding the process of history and will not abandon those whom He loves. The Hebrew believed that history began with creation and will end at the final judgment. But for the Christian the Incarnation was the decisive event, the middle from

Become flesh

INCARNATION   John 1-1

which the beginning and the end must be understood. The incarnation of Jesus Christ interpreted the whole of human history. It puts everything else into perspective.

Unlike other ancient religions that were rooted in mythologies, abstract concepts, or the cycles of nature, the Judeo-Christian faith offered itself to the world as a saving revelation mediated through historical events. The Old and New Testaments are held together by the bond of revelatory history. They are not history for history's sake but an inspired record of divine activity in history. The revelation of God and His purpose within the context of history is offensive to many, the scandal of Christianity, for it sets the revelation of God within the realm of time and space, flux and change. It means that God's activity on our behalf, and our activity on the behalf of others, must take place within the realm of the temporal and the mundane.

Historical narrative has always been the Judeo-Christian mode of knowing God's activity. It is also the place and the condition under which we fulfill God's purpose for our lives. Christians cannot do the work and will of God in the world without getting their hands dirty. The Holy Spirit does not take us out of our historical narrative but transforms and empowers us within it so that we can fulfill our mission in the world. Jesus revealed God's pupose for us when he prayed, "I do not pray that thou [Father] wouldst take them [Jesus' disciples] out of the world, but that thou shouldst keep them from the evil one . . . . As thou didst send me into the world, so I have sent them into the world" (John 17:15, 18). God's activity on our behalf has been in the realm of the human community. This is where we must act on behalf of those for whom we are called and to whom we are sent. He sets us apart for His service but not apart from those for whom God has already expressed concern in Jesus Christ. The locus of our work as Christians is the here and now. The Holy Spirit equips and enables us with power for the purpose of serving the needs of this world. God's purpose in freeing us from sin's bondage is that we might be free for the earthly task of reconciling others. It is in the realm of the earthly that God gives our lives eternal significance.

This does not mean that we become more effective in this world by ceasing to think of the other world. On the contrary, we find both earthly and heavenly meaning only when we begin with the heavenly perspective. The sense of eternity in what we do is what gives perspective and value to the earthly task. The point is that we must not forget the importance of what we have been called to do now nor diminish the sacredness of ordinary relationships and callings.

This emphasis comes through very clear in the theology of Martin Luther. It was a tenet of his theology that made it fresh and relevant for Luther's day and for our own. He reminded Christians that what they do in their homes is worth as much in the sight of God as if they did it in heaven for Him. We serve Christ through our neighbor. The place where the Christian life is made manifest is in relationships between husbands and wives, parents and children, tradesmen and customers, masters and servants, princes and people, teachers and students. It is revealed in our daily actions toward friends, strangers, and enemies. It is seen in our attitude toward rich and poor, learned and ignorant, high and low. Christians are freed for the purpose of serving others. Service is our responsibility. In Jesus Christ God accepts us and enables us to live out that acceptance by accepting ourself and others.

John Wesley once said that God is made visible to us in our neighbor. Serving God through one's neighbor is not always easy. Oftentimes it entails pain and hardship, but this is part of our solidarity with a fallen human race. What Christians have to strengthen them in times of trial and suffering is the life and hope of the risen Lord who also lived for others. They are assured by the Word that His grace will always be sufficient. During periods of hardship and stress we must not always depend upon our feelings. God's grace is not dependent upon the fickleness of our experiences or our feelings of His grace. God's grace is steadfast and continuous because it is grounded in the faithfulness of God to His promises. The Word of promise and the work of the Holy Spirit belong together, for both come forth from the divine purpose. What God promises in His Word, the Spirit will be faithful to perform.

Protestant bodies have traditionally recognized the Word and the sacraments as continuous means of grace, as signs of God's steadfast love and fidelity toward His people. The grace of God does not come only through crisis experiences when our feelings of His grace are heightened. Grace is constantly being appropriated to us as we remember the promises that are contained in the Word and the sacraments. Christians do well to remember this. But Pentecostals are also aware of God's sovereignty over history, and this means that God is free to work as He wills. God binds Himself to His Word, but His purposes are not always accomplished according to our fixed patterns of worship or our categories of thought. The church is always struggling to keep up with what the Spirit is doing, much like the early church was in the Book of Acts. The church ought always to acknowledge the "Godness" of God and adjust its thoughts and structures to Him. The church in history has always to do with the "living" God.

FINDING GOD'S "WHY" TO LIVE FOR

Purposeful living depends upon our discovering God's "why" for our lives. Victor Frankl, the Viennese psychiatrist who was a prisoner in a Nazi concentration camp during World War II, observed that the driving force within the prisoners was their search for meaning. When life is stripped to the bone, when all questions except ultimate questions seem trivial, Frankl discovered that what men want most is an answer to the "why" of life and death. Those who found a why to live for, Frankl reports, were much more likely to survive than those who did not. Frederich Nietzsche, the German philosopher who never found a why to live for, wrote in a poem entitled "Searching for God" that, "He who has a 'why' to live for can bear almost any 'how.'" Jean-Paul Sartre, the French existentialist who was himself an atheist, confessed that man's greatest need is for meaning. In an ambiguous world men "stalk for meaning," Sartre wrote, like hungry beasts searching for prey.

The grace of salvation means divine forgiveness and the promise of eternal life. But it also means personal fulfillment and meaning for the present. Salvation means new existence, new life in the Spirit. The purpose we find through redemption was made possible through God's purposeful work in creation. In creation the Spirit of God moved upon the face of the waters and brought forth an orderly world out of chaos (Genesis 1:2). From the material, physical stuff of the created order, the dust of the ground, God formed the first man and breathed life into his nostrils (Genesis 2:7). As a potter molds the clay according to his own design, the Creator God molded man and animated his being with His own Spirit (ruach). In creation God implanted a quest within man for God that only His Spirit can satisfy. God began His quest for man by inciting man to a quest for God. The Holy Spirit is God from whom man comes and by whom man returns to God. If God sought man but man did not seek God, or if man sought God and God did not seek man, the quest would be fruitless. But the quest is not fruitless because God has placed the impulse for eternity within us, and it keeps alive the desire for our true country. Augustine called this quest for God man's "restless heart." John Calvin called it man's "sense of the divine." It is this search for meaning and fulfillment in God that gives us a "why" for which to live and die.

FINDING IDENTITY THROUGH RECONCILIATION

The human spirit is man's God-given capacity for communion and fellowship with God. But it is also man's capacity for rebellion against God. Man's potential for greatness and his potential for evil are rooted in the same source—his freedom. The great tragedy of the human race has been man's refusal to bow before the majesty of God. Since Adam and Eve, man has been in rebellion against God and His purpose. The creature who was created to love, serve, glorify, and "enjoy God forever" lives estranged from his Creator. The human pair whom God created to enjoy the delights of the Garden desired one more thing—to be free and independent of God. Like the prodigal son, they turned their back on the Father and left their home. In doing so, God ceased to be the center of their life. They lost their standing with God; His image in man was marred. Instead of reflecting God's image, the sinful self-centeredness of man manifested itself in various forms of pride and lust.

The dilemma of fallen man was his bondage to sin. He could no more change his sinful nature than a leopard could change its spots. The creature who had received life from the life-giving Spirit was now dead in sin. God's image was distorted. Man's hope for a new beginning, a rediscovery of himself and his purpose, depended upon God's gracious initiative. Reconciliation through Jesus Christ was God's means of reestablishing man's identity.

A knowledge of man's sinful condition helps us understand the Spirit's work in regeneration and reconciliation. The evangelical message of the Bible centers in the fact that the Holy Spirit graciously convicts us of sin and frees our will so that we are enabled to cooperate with God's grace. Grace is a matter of God's coming to meet us and engaging us at the point of our freedom. The redemption that Christ has provided through His atoning sacrifice is efficaciously appropriated to us through the Holy Spirit. But it is more than a fact. It is an encounter. The truth of this personal encounter is not an "it" but a "thou." When the Holy Spirit encounters the human spirit in the work of regeneration we receive the adoption as sons of God. The Holy Spirit makes us aware of sonship through our experience of God as Father. Through personal encounter God becomes more to us than a cosmic force. He becomes a loving heavenly Father.

The same Spirit who moved upon the face of the deep moves in the human heart to recreate us after God's image. The life-giving Spirit that breathed life into man at creation gives new life to those who believe in Jesus Christ. In Jesus Christ God reclaims us for Himself. Through the power of the Holy Spirit God breaks the power of sin that holds us. On the level of personal choice each person must consciously choose to cooperate with or reject the drawing and convicting power of the Holy Spirit. He will not convert us against our will. But neither does He allow His purpose for us to be frustrated for lack of His own gracious action. God wills that we become the temple of the Holy Ghost. The Creator Spirit prepared us for this indwelling in creation. Through Christ's redeeming work the Holy Spirit now makes it a reality in our lives.

Any trip to the local bookstore will confirm that in our contemporary society the emphasis is upon self-helps and self-actualization. Pop-psychology and success books are having a field day. Secular humanisms attempt to define the meaning of life without any recourse to God's design. But all man-centered deviations from the divine plan are self-defeating. The meaning of human life— what it is and what God meant it to be—can only be defined by Jesus Christ. He is the key to our self-understanding. No other model will do. Jesus Christ revealed God, but He also revealed the meaning of our humanity. For He was the God-man. He was the perfectly whole man who revealed God's intention for the human family.

God's will is that we become fully human after the model of Jesus Christ. Spirituality does not involve our being lifted out of our humanity or human conditions. The test of true spirituality is our being enabled by the Holy Spirit to reflect Jesus Christ under human conditions. This is life lived according to the Spirit. God does not separate wholeness and holiness. In Christ, we are made whole and holy as the Holy Spirit actualizes those possibilities for which we were created. Spiritual maturity is our growing up in Him so that His character is reflected in us. God wills to be housed in us. "Do you not know," Paul asked the Corinthians, "that your body is the temple of the Holy Spirit within you, which you have from God? You are not your own; you were bought with a price. So glorify God in your Body" (1 Corinthians 6:19). The Christian cannot live according to the norm of sinful lusts because of the sanctity of the body. When we misuse the body we defile the temple of the Holy Spirit. Self-indulgences such as illicit sexual relations, alcohol and drug abuse, gluttony, immodesty, and the like have no place in the life of the Christian. Our bodies were meant to be an instrument for the service and honor of the Lord.

LIFE TOGETHER IN THE BODY OF CHRIST

There is a personal relationship with God, and there is a personal ethic that is appropriate for Christians. But one must also remember that purposeful living for the Christian means life together in the body of Christ. Fellowship with God is personal, but it is not private. God has bound us together in one body. Together, Christians share in the sufferings, the struggles, the joys, and the promises of the Church.

Jesus Christ did not come into the world to preach a new philosophy as much as He did to establish a new set of relationships. It is in the body of Christ that we learn these relationships. All relationships outside of Christ tend to deteriorate, to gravitate toward exploitation and oppression. "If we do not have Christ the Lord as our God," Dietrich Bonhoeffer once noted, "we will have ourselves as tyrants." In the Church, Jesus Christ is Lord. But He is not like the selfish and greedy lords of this world. Jesus never attempted to dominate and oppress others. He was the kind of Lord who served. In the body of Christ we are expected to live by a different set of relationships than that of the world. Christians are expected to prefer one another, to live by a law of mutual submission. Family members are to honor and respect each other, not to dominate or provoke. Christians ought to be the best citizens in the community and the nation because of their desire to serve others.

It is in the body of Christ that we learn not to separate individual experience(s) from the life and faith of the covenant community. Life in the Spirit cannot be separated from its communal form. In the Old Testament the Spirit moved upon particular persons for specific tasks, but the Spirit's work has always related to the welfare and advancement of the covenant community. Special experiences with God are highly valued, but they are not meant to result in states of religious self-centeredness in which the individual and his emotions become central. Preoccupation with one's own experiences inevitably results in moral insensitivity, social irresponsibility, and loss of community. When we descend into ourselves, and disconnect ourselves from other people, we soon lose sight of God's broader purpose. Life under God in the community of the faithful is more than spiritual euphoria or an emotional jab to keep one happy.[2] It is unity and love, in the body of Christ, under the authority of the Word of God. The edification of the whole body is what is most important.

Christians discover their identity and their calling as they relate to the body. Christ restores our rightful identity through the work of reconciliation, but He then makes us His partners for the reconciliation of others. Through the power of the Holy Spirit we become extensions of Jesus Christ in the world. Our individuality becomes a part of Christ's body in its totality, and we become the this-worldly form of Christ's existence in the world. All do not have the same gifts or the same function in the body, but all are vitally important to its functioning properly. No member of the body can say to another, "we have no need of you." For every member is gifted by the Holy Spirit for that place and that task that God would have them fill in the body of Christ.

LIVING A FRUITFUL AND PRODUCTIVE LIFE

It has never been God's will for our lives to be barren and unfruitful. God wills that our lives bear much fruit. If we are to be productive and fruit-bearing Christians, however, we must be empowered by the Holy Spirit. This truth is born out in both the Old and New Testaments.

In the Old Testament God's Spirit moved mightily upon those whose ministries and vocations were joined

If you don't use it, you lose it.

to the destiny of the covenant community. Natural abilities and skills were not enough. The "arm of the flesh" was not Israel's hope. Israel needed leaders in whom the Spirit of God could work, men empowered by the Holy Spirit to lead the people of God according to the divine purpose. Consequently, judges, kings, statesmen, prophets, and priests were anointed and empowered by the Spirit of God.

We easily miss the point in the story of Samson if we think that the Spirit arbitrarily settled upon Samson so that he could display supernormal strength in "tearing the lion" or in "carrying the gates of Gaza." Samson was the champion of Israel. God's Spirit was bestowed upon Samson because God's purpose required it in the conquest of Israel's enemy, the Philistines. The judges were divinely appointed men and women upon whom the Spirit was bestowed in a special manner for the purpose of leading and judging Israel. When Israel's leaders were empowered and led by the Spirit of God, the people were well served by common men who were not ordinarily thought of as national leaders. Israel's need for leadership and skill was always found in Spirit-empowered men.

The story of Bezalel and Oholiab is another case in point (Exodus chapter 31). Again, the point is easily missed if we take the account of the Spirit filling these craftsmen with wisdom, understanding, knowledge, and workmanship to simply mean that the Spirit sharpened their skills. The Holy Spirit certainly can and does sharpen skills, but the lesson to be learned from this story focuses upon the building of the Tabernacle which served Israel as a medium for divine revelation. Through the Tabernacle, and the form of worship that God prescribed for its use, a larger purpose was served. God's redemptive purpose for the nation was being revealed. When the Spirit filled Bezalel and Oholiab with special wisdom and skills, God revealed to the nation that all work could be divinely blessed and humanly meaningful if it furthered God's purpose for the people.

In Greek mythology there is a story about Sisyphus, a legendary king of Corinth, who so offended the gods

To Build The Tabernacle

that he was condemned for all eternity to roll a great boulder to the top of a mountain. According to the myth, the gods had so arranged things that each time Sisyphus neared the top of the mountain the boulder would roll back down to the bottom and poor Sisyphus would have to start all over again. The story of Sisyphus is a classic portrayal of the kind of endless, purposeless effort that so many put into life. Futile and unproductive labor produces in us a sense of meaninglessness. It is important that our activity be purposeful, just as God's activity is purposeful. Much of human life centers in our work. It is important to know that God wants to take our occupations, our work, and use it to further an eternal purpose. When our lives and our work have been dedicated to God, the Holy Spirit can take everyday activities and use them as He did Bezalel's and Oholiab's. Like Sisyphus, we may feel at times that we are only rolling boulders up a mountain, but if our work has been dedicated to God and His kingdom we can be assured that He will use the boulders we bring to Him to build an edifice at the top of the mountain that will last forever.

In the Old Testament the Holy Spirit's activity was more noticeable in the lives and ministries of those responsible for the nation's welfare. Israel's kings were anointed with oil, which symbolized the anointing of the Spirit, and set apart for the responsibility of ruling the people in accordance with the established covenant (1 Samuel 10:1; 16:3, 13; 2 Samuel 5:3; 1 Kings 1:34; 19:15; 2 Kings 9:3). Prophets and priests were anointed for religious tasks (Exodus 30:30; 40:13-15; Leviticus 8:12, 30; 16:32; 1 Kings 19:16). The duties of the altar and the responsibility of proclaiming the Word of the Lord were more than perfunctory or professional tasks. There could be no true prophecy, intercession, or worship apart from the work of the Holy Spirit. The anointing of the Spirit was necessary for every ministering office. As Zechariah reminded the people, it is "not by might, nor by power, but by my spirit, says the Lord of hosts" (Zechariah 4:6).

E. F. Scott, biblical scholar of a generation ago, noted

in his writings that more and more Israelites seemed to yearn for a closer personal fellowship with God through the Spirit in the later stages of Hebrew history. This desire appeared in the later Old Testament books as the chief end of life. David's prayer for repentance, "Take not thy holy spirit from me" (Psalm 51:11) became increasingly familiar in the experience of other Israelites as they discovered that the God who dwells in the heavens would also dwell in their hearts. Like David, who implored God's forgiveness because he desired a restored fellowship with God through the Holy Spirit, more and more Israelites wanted to serve God not for what they could receive from Him but for the assurance that He was near.[3]

The promise of a fuller fellowship with God through the Spirit in the age to come was a highlight in the message of the later Old Testament prophets. Ezekiel prophesied that the Spirit would give Israel new life in the future when the land and the people would be restored (Ezekiel chapter 37). Jeremiah spoke of a new covenant that God would write upon the heart (Jeremiah chapter 31). Individual responsibility and a more personal communion with God through the Spirit were anticipated for the New Age.

Isaiah prophesied that the Spirit would rest upon a Messiah king and anoint Him with power. A Spirit-anointed Messiah would usher in the New Age (Isaiah 11:1-3; 61:1-3). In the New Age God would bring to completion through a Spirit-anointed Messiah what He had begun through His covenant people Israel. But Joel, the prophet of Pentecost, foresaw an even greater outpouring of the Holy Spirit. He prophesied that the Holy Spirit would be poured out "on all flesh" so that all could be prophets and priests (Joel 2:28). Joel foresaw a messianic people upon whom the Messiah would pour out the Holy Spirit. Every person could then be Spirit empowered and productive in the work of the kingdom of God. Every man and woman could be a prophet and a priest unto God. The Apostle Peter announced on the Day of Pentecost that what they had received was what Joel had promised (Acts 2:16-18). Pentecost represented the beginning of a productive and fruit-bearing witness to Jesus Christ. So much so that Luke tells us, "The Lord added to their number day by day" (Acts 5:14).

It is God's will for the church today to grow and be productive. But real growth in the Church of Jesus Christ cannot be something that results from human ingenuity and strategy. The church must have a plan; it must have a strategy. But it must be one that is centered in the work of the Holy Spirit for He alone can convict the world of sin, of righteousness, and of judgment (John 16:8). He alone can bring members into the body of Christ. We are His instruments. Through Him, we can be productive and fruit-bearing Christians. We can become instruments of God's self-disclosure in Jesus Christ. This is the purpose for which God empowers us.

FOOTNOTES

[1]Diogenes Allen, *The Traces of God*, (Cambridge, Massachusetts: Cowley Publications, 1981), p. 8.

[2]For an excellent critique of the kind of religious experience that enthrones the self, see Will Herberg's *Protestant-Catholic-Jew*, (New York: Doubleday and Co., 1960), pp. 254-272.

[3]E. F. Scott, *The Spirit in the New Testament*, (London: Hodder and Stoughton), pp. 42, 43.

Grow + GO

To feed + Read
+
Lead + Seed and
meet The Need

Chapter 2

Christ-Centered Living

Finding the Proper Focus *in on your purpose*

The Protestant Bible has sixty-six books with two major divisions, the Old and the New Testaments. But it has one common theme that brings all of the diversity into one magnificent unity. That common theme is God and His purpose. In the New Testament we have the completion of the earlier process which was begun in the Old Testament. The revelation of God and His purpose is carried to completion in Jesus Christ. He is the central fact in the New Testament. The message connected to that fact is that "God was in Christ reconciling the world to himself." In Jesus Christ the person and purpose of God are absolutely and perfectly revealed. This is the primary truth with which Christians must concern themselves. Creation, Fall, Promise and Prophecy, the Coming of Christ in the fullness of time, His life, Death, Resurrection, Ascension, the Coming of the Holy Spirit, the Church, the spreading of the Gospel, the Second Coming, and the final Consummation—all are directly related to this central truth.

There are many variations of the one theme, just as there are secondary themes of great importance. But secondary themes ought never to obscure or usurp the truth of that which is primary. Any doctrine or experience that is not grounded in God's purpose as it is revealed in Jesus Christ cannot be Christian in either

33

precept or practice. The doctrine of the Holy Spirit is so important precisely because it finds its focus in Jesus Christ. His primary function is to witness to Jesus. It is only through the Holy Spirit that Jesus Christ can be experienced and understood.

One must take seriously the truth of the Holy Spirit while realizing that the Holy Spirit is not the center of Christian revelation. What the Holy Spirit does is set the center of truth, that center being the truth of Christ as we find it in the New Testament. And yet, the Holy Spirit does more than set the center; He makes possible our relation to Jesus Christ who is the center.

GOD'S GRACIOUS PROVISION IN JESUS CHRIST

In his classic work, *God Was in Christ,* Donald Baillie noted the paradox of grace that lies at the very heart of the biblical message. "The God in whom Christians believe," Baillie said, "is . . . the One who gives us what He demands of us, provides the obedience that He requires; so that we are constrained to acknowledge . . . the paradox of grace, expressed in the confession: 'I . . . yet not I, but the grace of God.' "[1] In Jesus Christ God has graciously provided all that He requires of us. Through the first-man Adam, man lost everything. Sin and death entered the world and all men came under its power. Through the second-man Adam, Jesus Christ, everything that was lost has been regained. Righteousness and life are ours in Jesus Christ (Romans 5:12-21).

Through His saving life, death, and resurrection Jesus Christ fulfilled all that the Law and righteousness of God require. As our vicarious substitute, He lived, and died, and rose again for us. The redemptive plan which God purposed for us was accomplished through two great acts of humility: Incarnation and Atonement.

Incarnation literally means God's "becoming flesh." The most concise expression of this great truth comes to us from John's Gospel, "And the Word was made flesh, and dwelt among us, and we beheld his glory, the glory as of the only begotten of the Father, full of grace and truth" (John 1:14). The term "Word" that is used here expresses the disclosure of the wisdom of God communicated to us in Jesus Christ. The term "flesh" refers to the human conditions under which the Word appeared and lived. Under the conditions of full humanity, the divine Son of God entered into and participated fully in man's history that He might redeem us from the curse of the Law. Jesus fulfilled all that God's law of love required. He fulfilled the Law perfectly because He loved perfectly. He lived, loved, taught, healed, and forgave as no man ever had. He was tempted to compromise God's purpose, to turn His back on His divinely appointed vocation, but He never yielded. He was faithful and obedient until the end. In emphasizing that Christ died for us, we oftentimes neglect the fact that Christ lived for us. Jesus Christ lived for us so that His life might be manifest in our mortal bodies (2 Corinthians 4:10, 11). Dying for Christ might actually be easier sometimes than living for Christ. But what Christ most often calls us to do is to live for Him, to make ourselves His living sacrifice (Romans 12:1).

The penalty for man's sin was death, and Jesus died for our sins (Romans 3:24-26; 1 Corinthians 15:3). Jesus' death was no mere accident; Jesus was not some martyr slain for a religious cause. He was the lamb of God slain from the foundation of the world for man's sin. Hundreds of years before Christ was born the Prophet Isaiah declared that God would make his soul an offering for sin (Isaiah 53:10). Christ was literally God's sacrifice for sin (Romans 3:25; 1 John 2:2; 4:10; Hebrews 2:17). He was the sacrifice which all other Old Testament sacrifices anticipated, the sacrifice in which all other sacrifices were fulfilled. Christ was the price, the ransom, that God paid in order to reconcile fallen man, to bring man back into atonement [at/one/ment] with God.

Through Christ's death God offers us life. He died for us that we might live for Him. And yet it is not our old life that is lived but His life that is lived in us through the power of the Holy Spirit. The paradox of Christianity is that it offers us life through death. We cannot expect to live for Christ until we are willing to die to self. There is an altar of sacrifice upon which we too must offer ourselves. "I am crucified with Christ," Paul said, "nevertheless I live; yet not I, but Christ liveth in me: and the life which I now live in the flesh I live by the faith of the Son of God, who loved me, and gave himself for me" (Galatians 2:20).

If, on the cross, He was "delivered up for our offenses," Paul said, Christ was on the third day "raised again for our justification" (Romans 4:25). Jesus' resurrection was a victory for us over death, hell, and the grave. It is the basis of our hope for life beyond the grave. But just as importantly, it is the newness of life in which we now live. This is what our water baptism symbolizes. We are lowered into the water, symbolizing death to the old life. But we are raised up out of the water, symbolizing the newness of resurrection life which we have in Jesus Christ. In the Christian life we live out the meaning of our water baptism (Romans 6:1-8).

APPROPRIATION THROUGH THE HOLY SPIRIT

After many post-resurrection appearances, Jesus left His disciples with one great commission and one great promise. The commission was to "Go . . . and make disciples of all nations, baptizing them in the name of the Father, and of the Son, and of the Holy Ghost, teaching them to observe all that I have commanded you." The promise was, "I am with you always, to the close of the age" (Matthew 28:19, 20; RSV). The lingering question, however, was "how" Jesus would be with His disciples, scattered throughout the world, after His ascension. This perplexed Jesus' disciples. They were greatly troubled at the prospect of Jesus being taken from them.

After His ascension, one hundred and twenty faithful disciples remembered the final command of Jesus and hurried obediently to an upper room in Jerusalem. They remembered that Jesus had told them they would be witnesses to what they had seen and heard. The promised Holy Spirit would clothe them with power so that they would be able to spread the good news in Jerusalem,

Judea, Samaria, and to the ends of the earth (Luke 24:48, 49; Acts 1:8). As they went, Christ would be with them as He promised, in the person and power of the Holy Spirit.

As a result of what happened at Pentecost, the disciples of Jesus made two startling discoveries. First, the divine presence of which they were so aware while the Master was with them "in the flesh" was again with them through the Holy Spirit. Second, even those who had not known Jesus in the flesh could experience the power and presence of Jesus through faith. As Jesus' disciples continued telling the story and others believed in Him, the presence of Jesus continued to be experienced.[2] The salvation that God had graciously provided through Christ's life, death, and resurrection was now being appropriated to believers through the Holy Spirit.

An experience of Christ was not an experience that depended upon a knowledge of Jesus in the flesh. Many who had never seen or heard Him personally received Jesus by faith. Yet God's transforming grace in their life was no less real than that Jesus' own disciples had experienced. It was just as full, as deep, and as transforming as if Jesus was personally present to bestow it. The truth, of course, was that Jesus was present in the person and power of the Holy Spirit. Through the Holy Spirit Jesus would be with all believers until the end of the age when He would physically return to receive His own.

Making Christ present and available through the Holy Spirit was a further stage in God's redemptive purpose. But it was not an experience that was independent of the historical Jesus. It all depended upon Him. Had Jesus not come, lived, and died the reality of His presence could not have been experienced. But because He had come, the Holy Spirit could now take the things of Christ and show them to those who were receptive to the living Christ.

JESUS AND THE HOLY SPIRIT

Thoughts about the Holy Spirit tend to be scattered until they find cohesion in our understanding of Jesus

Christ. In the Scriptures, Christ is like a magnetic field around which all else arranges itself. He is the central truth upon which we must focus. God does not reveal Himself to be other than we know Him already in Jesus Christ. All that we know about God in the now, or will ever know in the hereafter, will accord with what we know about Him in Christ.

The God who is revealed to us in Scripture as Father, Son and Holy Spirit is one God, not three Gods. Consequently, the Scriptures bring the Holy Spirit into the closest possible relationship with the one God who was in Christ reconciling the world unto Himself. Because Jesus Christ is the focus of New Testament revelation, the Spirit is always brought into close relationship to Him. This does not obscure the clear teaching of Scripture regarding the Holy Spirit's person or divinity. The Holy Spirit is a divine person in the Trinity, just like the Father and the Son. Yet, the truth regarding His divine person is never allowed to detract from the truth of God's unity or the truth of God's person as it is revealed in Jesus Christ. The Holy Spirit hides Himself in Christ because they are unified in purpose.

Still the New Testament focus upon Jesus Christ does not detract from the essential activity of the Holy Spirit. For it is in the power of the Spirit that Jesus accomplishes the purpose of God. The Holy Spirit is the Spirit of truth and revelation. He is the one who takes the things of Christ and shows them to us.

WHAT THE GOSPELS TEACH ABOUT THEIR RELATIONSHIP

The work of the Spirit is always in perfect harmony with God's purpose in Christ. There is no individualized ego in the Spirit which seeks for a Spirit-consciousness that is distinct from a knowledge of Christ. References to the Spirit acting upon Jesus' disciples generally assign that action to the time after Jesus' ascension. As long as Jesus was with the disciples, attention was fixed upon Christ as the revelation of the Father. Jesus spoke of the importance of the Spirit's coming. He also noted how essential the Spirit's work would be, but the Spirit's work always presupposed the work of the incarnate Christ. The Spirit's essential relationship to Christ can be seen in those things which Christ himself taught concerning the Holy Spirit in the Synoptic Gospels:

(1) He taught that the Holy Spirit is a gift whom the Father will give to those who ask Him (Luke 11:9-13).

(2) He promised that when His followers were put on trial before human authorities the Holy Spirit would assist them by teaching them what to say (Luke 12:11, 12; Mark 13:9-11; Mathew 10:16-20).

(3) He commanded the disciples to baptize believers in the name of the Father, the Son, and the Holy Spirit (Matthew 28:19).

(4) He commanded the disciples to wait in Jerusalem until they were clothed with the power of the Holy Spirit which would make them witnesses (Luke 24:49; Acts 1:8).

It is noteworthy that none of these texts teach a Spirit-consciousness that is unrelated to Christ and the Christian mission. Furthermore, the special work of the Holy Spirit is not generally referred to in any situation where Christ himself was present.[3] As long as Christ was present, He was their "helper" and "advocate." When He departed, the Holy Spirit would come in a special way as "another" comforter (paraclete).

The Spirit was the promise of the New Age. He would come in power after Christ's departure to bear witness to Christ and to appropriate to believers the life and grace provided through Christ's atoning work. The Holy Spirit was for the disciples' advantage then because Christ's death and resurrection made possible the Spirit's witness and work (John 16:6, 7). Until Christ ascended and was glorified, the Spirit had no need to come as He came at Pentecost.

The close relation of the Holy Spirit to the redemptive purpose of God, as an eschatological gift, is made clear in John's Gospel. In the Fourth Gospel the work of the Spirit always presupposes the death and resurrection of Jesus, either through the use of future tenses (as in chapters 14-16), by close association with water (cleansing) and flesh (the Lord's Supper which would have special significance after Christ's death; (John 3:5; 6:63), or by direct statement from the lips of Jesus (John 7:39). In John's Gospel, the Spirit was "not yet" at work, as at Pentecost, except in Jesus himself. This is consistent with what we observe in the synoptic Gospels. Jesus is the bearer of the Holy Spirit. He promises that the Holy Spirit will be given after His glorification (that is, after He has been crucified, resurrected and ascended): "Now this he said about the Spirit, which those who believed in him were to receive; for as yet the Spirit had not been given, because Jesus was not yet glorified" (John 7:39). The coming of the Holy Spirit presupposed the finished work of Christ on the earth because His work was directly connected with Jesus' work.

In the well-known paraclete passages, in the parting discourses of the Fourth Gospel (Chapters 14-16), the close relationship between Jesus and the Spirit is maintained. Jesus promises His disciples that after His ascension and glorification the Father will send the Paraclete, the Holy Spirit, in His name (John 14:26). The use of the term "paraclete" is restricted in the New Testament to the Johannine writings (John 14:16, 17; 14:26; 15:26; 16:7 cf. 13: 1 John 2:1). In 1 John 2:1 the term is applied to the exalted Jesus who acts as an advocate before the Father for those who sin. Elsewhere it is applied to the Holy Spirit. It is unfortunate that the term paraclete was translated "comforter" in the widely read Authorized Version of the Bible (KJV). The Holy Spirit is indeed the Comforter. And perhaps the translators were prone to identify the Holy Spirit with Jesus' desire to comfort His disciples in the parting discourses. But biblical scholars are in general agreement that the term has a much broader meaning than our contemporary understanding of "comforter." The term could just as well be translated "helper," "supporter," "advocate," or "counselor."

In John 14:16 the Holy Spirit is described as "another" Paraclete which, of course, implies that Jesus himself is a Paraclete (John 2:1). The Paraclete is said to be given by the Father at the Son's request. In John 14:26 the Father is said to send the Paraclete in Christ's name. In John 15:26 Christ sends the Paraclete from the Father, and He proceeds from the Father. In John 16:7 Christ is said to send the Paraclete. Scholars generally agree that John intends no significant difference between these expressions. Both Christ and the Holy Spirit are the believer's Paraclete. Both serve God's redemptive purpose. As Christ bears witness to the Father, the Holy Spirit bears witness to the Son.

It is the purpose of the "Spirit of truth" to bear witness to the truth, Jesus Christ (John 1:17; 14:6; 14:17). "When the Spirit of truth comes," Jesus said, "he will guide you into all the truth; for he will not speak on his own authority, but whatever he hears he will speak, and he will declare it to you" (John 16:13, 14). Jesus also promised that the Holy Spirit would aid the disciples in remembering His teachings and sayings (John 14:26). Since the Holy Spirit is vitally related to prophecy and the inspiration of Scripture (2 Peter 1:20), it is not surprising that the Spirit would supernaturally aid those whose responsibility it was to bear a faithful witness to Christ in remembering and reproducing Jesus' words. A sound doctrine of Scripture depends upon a strong doctrine of the Holy Spirit.[4]

The sphere of the Spirit's witness is in believers. It ought not to be expected that the world will bear witness to Christ, for the world reacts negatively to Christ and rejects the Holy Spirit (John 14:17). Because it rejects the truth, the world is brought under judgment. The Spirit convicts the world for its false view of sin, righteousness, and judgment (John 16:8-11). The Spirit of truth in believers stands forever opposed to the spirit of error that is in the world. John does not teach that the Spirit's presence will be in those who reject Christ. God has demonstrated His love for the world in Jesus Christ (John 3:16). Those who reject God's love ought not to expect God's Spirit. The Holy Spirit is promised only to the committed people of God.

PAUL'S TEACHING

What we have said about the Spirit's relationship to Christ in the synoptic Gospels and in John's writings is also true for the Apostle Paul. Without confusing their work or their person, Paul brings Jesus and the Spirit into the closest possible relation. The Spirit cannot be separated from God's purpose that is revealed through the Cross and the empty tomb. In places, Paul scarcely distinguishes the Spirit from the risen Lord (Romans 8:9, 10). Why does he unite the Spirit with Christ so closely? Does Paul confuse Christ and the Spirit so as to deny the person of the Holy Spirit? The answer is that Paul does not. The "seeming identity" is really more of a dynamic relation than it is an identity of persons. Paul's stress throughout is that the Spirit cannot be severed from the Lord Christ himself without losing the meaning of Christian experience altogether.

Paul calls the Holy Spirit the Spirit of the Lord. The use of the preposition "of" designates the Spirit in relation to Christ, but it equally points to a distinction between them.[5] Influenced as Paul was by his background in the Old Testament and Rabbinic Judaism, he would never have endorsed any form of tritheism (that is, the belief in three gods). Paul was as devoted a monotheist as any Old Testament prophet. The Trinity, for Paul, was not a matter of mathematical statement about how three relates to one; nor was it a matter of speculative dogma. It was more of a confession about how God has made Himself known through revelation and experience. The one God who had been made known in Jesus Christ was known to Paul through the Holy Spirit. The objective fact of Christ is subjectively appropriated to experience through the Spirit. Where Christ has been made Lord, the outward fact penetrates to the inner heart of man and takes possession of him there. This is the work of the Spirit. "No one can say 'Jesus is Lord' except by the Holy Spirit," Paul says (1 Corinthians 12:3). This is why the communication of Christ cannot depend upon human eloquence or wisdom. Paul had no confidence in a knowledge of Christ that was "after the flesh" (that is, from a natural point of view, 2 Corinthians 5:16). He knew that the Spirit alone could open the inner apprehension of man and establish Christ as Lord in the heart.

KNOWING THE JESUS WHOM THE HOLY SPIRIT REVEALS

In the previous section I emphasized that the Holy Spirit is brought into the closest possible relation to the redemptive mission of Christ. Through the Holy Spirit, believers are effectually united to the Redeemer. A clear focus on the Holy Spirit requires an understanding of how He is bound to the Son. Whenever the Holy Spirit is at work, we can know that it is for the purpose of glorifying Jesus Christ. The close association, however, need not lead to a confusion of their persons. Scripture and experience make it possible to conceive of one God, existing in three persons.

The knowledge of the Trinity first arose as a datum of revelation and experience—not as a dogma of theology. The God who is revealed in Jesus Christ is made known and experienced through the Holy Spirit. But it is necessary to understand that the Christ to whom the Spirit bears witness is always the historical Jesus of Scripture, not a pneumatic or mysterious Christ removed from the realm of history and human conditions.

Søren Kierkegaard, the Christian existentialist, once commented that Jesus' contemporaries enjoyed no advantage over those of us who know Jesus from a truly spiritual point of view. Jesus' "contemporaries" are those who know Jesus after the Spirit.[6] There is something profoundly true about Kierkegaard's statement, but it also contains a dangerous half-truth. The Jesus whom the Spirit reveals to us is always the historical Jesus. Christians need to be clear about the kind of knowledge they can have of Christ.

The logic of a natural knowledge of Christ is clear enough. A Christ who cannot be seen cannot be known, and a Christ who cannot be known cannot be understood. And if Christ cannot be understood or known well enough to be loved and trusted then He cannot become the Lord of our life. It is equally important to recognize that truth and knowledge of Jesus Christ can never be authoritatively imposed nor effectively argued. Jesus' method was always to win persons through their own self-surrender, through their willful trust and devotion to His person. The responses which Christ willed to secure from other persons were never forced. They were motivated and inspired by the inward working of the Holy Spirit. William Barclay once observed that, "The acceptance of the will of God and . . . the Spirit of God go hand in hand." "But what," Barclay asked, "does the Holy Spirit have to do with our seeing, our knowing, our trusting, so that a total self-surrender results and Christ becomes Lord of one's life?"

According to biblical psychology, there is a spiritual seeing and a spiritual hearing that perceive and understand things which the normal senses cannot (Matthew 13:13-15; Mark 8:18). "Spiritual things," Paul says, "are spiritually discerned" (1 Corinthians 2:13). The medium for spiritual perception is man's spirit. The human spirit is man's invisible glory, a part of that which man possesses by reason of God's image in Him. Spiritual perception is different from and deeper than ordinary cognitive powers. The spiritual perception of which I speak does not belong to the natural man whose spirit is in rebellion against God. It cannot receive the things of God. In contrast to "dull ears" which cannot hear, and "eyes which cannot see" (Matthew 13:13-15), the Scriptures allude to a knowledge of God that results from the inward testimony and illumination of the Holy Spirit. Reference is made to eyes of the heart which have been enlightened (Ephesians 1:18), hearts which have been opened (Acts 16:14) or circumcised (Romans 2:29), of the veil being removed (2 Corinthians 3:15 ff.), of spiritual understanding (Colossians 1:9), of being able to hear and understand Christ (1 John 5:20; John 10:13).

Even among natural men, there are different levels of perception. As Bernard Ramm notes, "The cultured person enjoys a concert which may bore the farmer; the clever person sees the point of a barb, or the force of a satire, or the meaning of an illustration which eludes the ordinary person; the sensitive moral person sees the ethical issue in a situation which escapes the brutal man."[7] But the difference in the levels of perception which exist in the natural man and the spiritual man are deeper and more serious. While the farmer's perception of Beethoven may be relatively poor, compared to the trained musicologist, his musical sensibilities could improve through exposure and training. The natural man's perception, however, can never be made clear through training, cultural exposure, or religious intensity. Unless it is "illuminated" by the Holy Spirit to see and understand the things of Christ, the sin-darkened mind of man will never overcome the noetic effects of sin. The difference between natural and spiritual perception is one of no small significance.

Facts available to the same persons do not always produce the same results. Edwin Lewis, the great Methodist theologian of a generation ago, brilliantly illustrated this point from the New Testament: "Christ delivered a man from evil, and the judgment was passed, 'He casteth out demons by the prince of demons.' He called himself 'Son of God,' and many who heard it shrank from him in horror as a blasphemer. He hung on a cross, and the passers-by 'railed' and the chief priest 'mocked' and the rulers 'scoffed': they saw nothing but a crucified criminal. The tomb was found empty, and the authorities said: 'A stolen body' . . . on the Day of Pentecost some asked, 'What meaneth this?' And the answer came: 'These men are filled with new wine.'"[8] The same facts led men whose spirits had been touched by the Holy Spirit to different conclusions from those whose spirits had not.

Truths are not always of the same kind, but if they are truth they must come ultimately from the same source. There are, for example, truths which concern the very nature and meaning of existence itself. There are truths concerning events and their meaning. There are truths concerning relationships among persons and of man's relation to God. In every case, Jesus Christ is the ultimate interpretive key. Every truth, whether it be a truth of being, event, or relationship, can be given a different meaning from the one given in the New Testament.[9] Different men face the same facts but see them differently. The natural explanation for this difference of perception and understanding is what moderns call relativism. Relativism holds that there are no absolute truths with respect to ultimate realities and the fundamental issues of life. What is right and good must be humanly determined according to that which is right and good in every man's own eyes.

Christianity alone offers a release from the vicious circle of subjectivism and relativism which holds men captive to their own opinions and skepticisms regarding ultimate realities. It does so by announcing a set of absolutes. These absolute truths affirm God, all that God is, and the full and final revelation of God in Jesus Christ. These truths reveal what man is, and what he is meant to be. They teach us that every man is a sinner but that God has purposed that the power of sin be broken. These absolute truths tell us in what relation we were meant to stand to God and our fellowman. They teach us that agape love is the law of life, that through it we come into the fullness of life which Christ provides.[10]

Against all naturalisms, relativisms, evolutionisms, secularisms, or any other "ism" which teaches contrary to these truths, the New Testament offers us the absolute truth. But why do some see, hear, understand, and trust in these truths while others seemingly cannot? Why is it that some seemingly have an unshakable inward certainty while others remain so uncertain and skeptical? The late John Baillie once noted that for those who have never been confronted by God's revelation, as illumined and guaranteed by the Holy Spirit, "argument is useless, while to those who have it is superfluous."[11] This was professor Baillie's way of saying that the truth persuasion of the New Testament is in the Holy Spirit's illumination and assurance. The options are clear. One can either accept the illuminated truth when it comes and hold to it as something important and authoritative. Or, one can dismiss it as something imaginary and fictitious. In which case, Christian truth will no longer be held worthy of vital concern.

Our response to the inward guidance of the Holy Spirit can indeed lead us into a plenitude of truth, conviction, and persuasion, but our response does not determine the truthfulness and authority of the Word. Oxthodox theology has always insisted that inspired Scripture is true whether or not the individual receives it, or the church approves it. The Scriptures are the Word of God by virtue of their inspiration. Just as red is intrinsically red before you see it, and sugar is intrinsically sweet before you taste it, God's Word is true regardless of the subjective attitute one may assume toward it.[12] The truth and certainty of that which is announced to us in the New Testament is absolute and supremely authoritative. But its truth and power are made known to us through the inner witness of the Holy Spirit.

In the context of a discussion regarding uncertainty, Martin Luther once exclaimed: "The Holy Spirit is not a skeptic." The Holy Spirit breathes certainty. Through the Spirit, God bears bold witness to Jesus Christ.[13]

LIVING ACCORDING TO THE SPIRIT

The Apostle Paul knew that the truth of God in Jesus Christ must be spiritually apprehended. He had no confidence in a knowledge of Christ "after the flesh." Paul once thought of Christ as a man shamefully crucified, but after his conversion he came to know him as the risen Lord (2 Corinthians 5:16). Paul's judgments were no longer formed about Christ "according to the flesh"; they were formed according to what Paul described as the "mind of the Spirit" (Romans 8:4).

Paul's point is made more specific in his first letter to the Corinthians where he contrasts "spiritual men" with "natural men" who are blind to spiritual truths.

And we impart this in words not taught by human wisdom but taught by the Spirit, interpreting spiritual truths to those who possess the Spirit. The unspiritual [natural] man does not receive the gifts of the Spirit of God, for they are folly to him, and he is not able to understand them because they are spiritually discerned. The spiritual man judges all things, but is himself to be judged by no one (1 Corinthians 2:13-15).

Spiritual understanding is set in contrast to that which is perceived by the natural man. If one does not understand God and His saving purpose in light of the understanding that the Holy Spirit gives, he will understand him in light of the spirit of this world (Ephesians 2:2). There is no neutral understanding. Those things which are inaccessible to the natural man can be made known to the spiritual man.

Paul does not condemn the natural man because he lives his natural life "in flesh." The Christian is "flesh" too. The flesh is not inherently evil as the gnostics taught. It is not "flesh" *(sarx)* that Paul condemns, but life that is lived "according to the flesh" *(kata sarx)*. Life "according to the flesh" does not refer to that which is merely human, natural, and transitory; it refers to that sinful norm by which life is directed when life is lived devoid of the Spirit of God. Life "according to the flesh" is prompted by an attitude of sinful self-reliance.[14] It was characteristic of the Jew who boasted of the Torah and his own works-righteousness; it was characteristic of the Greek who boasted of his wisdom *(sophia)*. Only in the Lord did Paul make his boast. When Paul recalled the Christian message that he had preached to the church at Corinth, he wrote:

> When I came to you, brethren, I did not come proclaiming to you the testimony of God in lofty words or wisdom. For I decided to know nothing among you except Jesus Christ and him crucified. And I was with you in weakness and in much fear and trembling; and my speech and my message were not in plausible words of wisdom, but in demonstration of the Spirit and of the power, that your faith might not rest in the wisdom of men but in the power of God (1 Corinthians 2:1-5).

The Holy Spirit is our only access to heavenly wisdom. Our knowledge of God is dependent upon knowledge and wisdom mediated through the Holy Spirit (1 Corinthians 2:7; 2:13). But the content of that knowledge and wisdom is always the same. It is the wisdom of God that the Holy Spirit makes known to us through the Cross. The only Christ to whom the Spirit bears witness is the historical Jesus. He is not a pneumatic or phantom Christ, shrouded in gnostic mystery—but Jesus of Nazareth. The Christ of faith can never be separated from the Jesus of history. Paul never repudiated a "fleshly" Christ, only a knowledge of Christ that was "after the flesh" (Galatians 1:16; Romans 8:7).

THE INCARNATIONAL CHARACTER OF NEW TESTAMENT LIVING

In the Hellenistic world in which the New Testament had its setting there were so-called gnostics who claimed a "special knowledge" of truth reserved only for the spiritually elite. The special knowledge which gnostics claimed for themselves was not merely an intellectual or cognitive understanding. It involved a vision of God which supposedly gave an intimate personal insight into the realm of the ultimate. It was an intense and highly emotional experience, often accompanied by states of ecstasy. A gnostic believed that he could be delivered from the world, the flesh, and the realm of the earthly through this special form of spiritual knowledge. Death was considered the ultimate deliverance of the self from the body and its release into the heavenly world of light. But even in this present life the gnostic believed that the spark of light from the divine world could illumine him and give him salvation. Although his human nature presently remains bound to the earth, the gnostic was unconcerned because he believed that his essential spiritual self was deified through this secret redemptive knowledge. Consequently, the gnostic believed that to live "according to the Spirit" was to live above the stress and strain of this world. Gnostics tended to go in one of two extreme directions, toward asceticism and withdrawal from the world or toward libertinism and immorality.

Gnostic cults were widespread and influential; so they

constituted a serious threat to such fundamental Christian truths as the goodness of creation, the humanity of Christ, and bodily resurrection. In the New Testament writings, John tenaciously guarded the true humanity of Christ against the gnostic heresy (1 John 2:22; 4:2, 15; 5:1, 5-8; 2 John 7), and Paul defended bodily resurrection against gnostic tendencies in 1 Corinthians chapter 15. But the Gnostics were not easy to refute because many of them practiced ascetic, moralistic lifestyles, and when confronted with their errors they could always appeal to their morality and to their "higher" knowledge.

Gnostics, of one sort or another, have always been around. This is why one must be very careful in talking about "spiritual knowledge" and "hidden meanings." The gnostic tendency among pneumatics has always been a threat to the historical and incarnational character of the Christian faith. Regardless of its subtle forms which may make it sound lofty and superior, gnosticism always represents a distortion of that which is Christian. The New Testament writers resisted it, and so must we. They steadfastly held to the necessity of the inner illumination and witness of the Holy Spirit, but they never detracted from the historical and human character of the Christian life. If we ignore or diminish the historical and incarnational character of the faith, we lose sight of both Christ's purpose and our own. For the Christian is called to model his life after the historical Jesus who, in the power of the Holy Spirit, carried His commissioned task to completion. Christians today, like Christ, live and work under human conditions. The church must never be so earthly minded as to possess no heavenly wisdom, but it can ill afford to become so heavenly minded that it is of no earthly good. The task which Christ calls us to share with Him necessitates our involvement with people and their earthly problems.

A balanced perspective can be found in the Gospels where the Holy Spirit led Simon Peter to confess Jesus as "the Christ, the Son of the Living God" by revelation of the Father—not through "flesh and blood." Proofs and arguments never lead us to the truth that is in

Jesus Christ. He is the truth of revelation, the historical truth one comes to know through the inner witness of the Holy Spirit. Yet the Jesus to whom the Spirit gave an inward witness to Peter was the Jesus whom Peter knew in the flesh. It was not some mystical, pneumatic Christ. The historical personality in the gospel story is the same Christ who is our glorified Lord today.

If a revelation of God and His purpose could be known through "inward testimony," apart from the historical Jesus, then Christ lived for nothing and the Word was made flesh in vain. No "spiritual insight" or "hidden meaning" that is from God will ever lead us away from the historical, fleshly Jesus. The denial of flesh and incarnation is the spririt of Antichrist. Spiritual ecstasy is not the surest sign that the Spirit of God is in us. The surest sign is our testimony in word and deed to the incarnate Christ. John saw the dangers of the gnostic heresy and warned:

> Beloved, do not believe every spirit, but test the spirits to see whether they are of God; for many false prophets have gone out into the world. By this you know the Spirit of God: every spirit which confesses that Jesus Christ has come in the flesh is of God, and every spirit which does not confess Jesus is not of God. This is the spirit of antichrist, of which you heard that it was coming, and now it is in the world already (1 John 4:1-3).

The inward testimony of the Holy Spirit is absolutely essential to our being contemporaries of the historical Jesus, to our knowing Him and His purpose as the Holy Spirit would have us know Him. But we must also know that the inward working of the Holy Spirit is meant only to illumine and certify the objective truth of the historical Jesus whom we know from Scripture, never to create a mystical substitute for Him. Scripture is the Christian's final authority and objective standard of truth. It alone bears faithful witness to the historical Jesus. This is as Christ willed it. Jesus had many disciples and witnesses, but He specifically chose twelve men to be with him until the end. These men were to be authoritative eyewitnesses of His life, death, and resurrection. From these men and those closely associated with them, the Christian church received the divinely inspired Scriptures. Together, the Word and the Spirit provide the believer with a knowledge of God's person and purpose that is trustworthy and accurate. They provide the meaning and the power for Christ-centered living.

THE PURPOSE OF THE HOLY SPIRIT

Jesus Christ is the *raison d'etre* for understanding the doctrine of the Holy Spirit in the New Testament. There is an inseparable union between Christ and the Spirit because the purpose of the Spirit is to reveal Jesus Christ, the center and focus of Christian revelation. Christ is the key to understanding the meaning of the Spirit's activity, just as Christ's life is the key to understanding the meaning of our own. But just as importantly, it is the Holy Spirit that enables us to see and to be what God intends. Christians are called to be what Jesus Christ would be if He were on the earth today, living under human conditions. The truth is that Jesus Christ does live today, under human conditions, enfleshed in believers. We are His body. We become what Jesus was when we are empowered and led by the Holy Spirit. The Holy Spirit is the life-giving Spirit who appropriates and channels Christ's life and presence into the life of the believer. This is Christ-centered living.

There must be no evasion of the incarnational character of New Testament Christianity. There can be no separation between the "Christ of faith" and the "Jesus of history." Only the Holy Spirit can illumine our knowledge of Christ. Yet, the Christ who is Lord in our hearts is the Jesus of history after whom we are called to model our lives.

FOOTNOTES

[1]Donald Baillie, *God Was in Christ* (New York: Charles Scribner's Sons, 1948), pp. 114 ff., 145.

[2]Ibid., 144 ff., 153 ff.

[3]The one exception is John 20:22. New Testament scholars are divided over the interpretation of this verse. Many view it as John's

shortened account of Pentecost; others understand it in terms of a pre-Pentecost account of regeneration.

[4]Since the time of David Friedrich Strauss (1808-74), many biblical critics have questioned the "historical eyewitness" account of the longer discourses in John's Gospel. Strauss argued that it is contrary to the laws belonging to the human faculty of memory that long discourses, such as those of Jesus given in the Fourth Gospel, could have been faithfully recollected and reproduced. What Strauss failed to take into consideration was the supernatural aid that was rendered the human authors of Scripture by the Holy Spirit so that there would be a faithful witness to Christ.

[5]George S. Hendry also makes this observation in *The Holy Spirit in Christian Theology* (London: SCM, 1957), p. 25.

[6]For Kierkegäard's development of this theme see *Philosophical Fragments*, trans. David F. Swenson (Princeton: Princeton University Press, 1969), pp. 68 ff.

[7]Bernard Ramm, *Witness of the Spirit* (Grand Rapids, Michigan: Eerdmans, 1960), p. 37.

[8]Edwin Lewis, *A Philosophy of the Christian Revelation* (New York: Harper and Brothers, 1940), pp. 258, 259.

[9]Ibid., p. 139.

[10]Ibid., pp. 132-143.

[11]John Baillie, *Our Knowledge of God* (New York: Scribner, 1959), p. 132.

[12]Ramm, pp. 14, 16, 63.

[13]See G. C. Berkouwer, "The Spirit's Certainty," *Current Religious Thought* (October 22, 1965).

[14]Rudolf Bultmann, *Theology of the New Testament, Vol. I,* trans. Kendrick Grobel (New York: Scribner's, 1951), pp. 237, 238.

Chapter 3

The Divine Person of
The Holy Spirit

The Loss of the Holy Spirit's
Person in the Historic Church

The proper focus for Christian theology was established by Jesus himself when He asked His disciples, "Whom say ye that I am?" And Peter replied, "You are the Christ, the Son of the living God." It was appropriate for the church to focus first on the essential issue of Christ's person for He is the center and circumference of the gospel. He is the center of Christian revelation. Until Christians are sure about who Jesus is, they will not be sure of much else.

Pentecostals have traditionally embraced the teachings of the historic Ecumenical Creeds concerning Christ's person.[1] Most Christians believe Jesus' complete deity and humanity to be an essential affirmation of the Christian faith. What many fail to understand, however, is the importance of the person of the Holy Spirit who makes Christ real and present. The loss of the Spirit's person is tantamount to losing Christ.

The Holy Spirit's person has not been as clearly understood in the Christian church as the person of the Father and Son. In the Old Testament, emphasis was placed upon the Oneness of Jehovah God. The person of the Father was central. In the New Testament, attention focused upon Jesus Christ as the center of Christian revelation, but there was also a strong emphasis upon the Holy Spirit as the power of the New Age. History shows us, however, that as the post-apostolic church became more institutionalized and sacramentalized, the desire to experience the Holy Spirit's power and presence diminished. As it did, the church's recognition of the Holy Spirit's divine person became more of a traditional cnfession and less of a dynamic experience. When the Holy Spirit was allowed to work freely and spontaneously in the church, as He did in Acts, His person was readily acknowledged. When the church later sought to sacramentalize the Spirit and encapsulate Him within its institutional forms, it seemingly became less clear about His person.

As the Christian church moved into the second century, it continued to baptize in the Spirit's name as it did the Father's and Son's (Matthew 28:19). It continued to acknowledge the Spirit's person in worship according to the liturgical benediction found in Corinthians (2 Corinthians 13:17). But an acknowledgement of the Spirit's person in the church's liturgy and creeds could not substitute for an acknowledgement of His person in experience. The loss of the Spirit in personal experience was perhaps the greatest loss the Christian church has known. For in losing the Spirit, the church lost Christ. The temptation of the Roman Catholic church, after it became so sacramentalized and ecclesiastically structured, was to put itself in the place of Christ. Unfortunately, the church succumbed to the temptation.

The Protestant reformers saw many of the errors of Rome in the sixteenth century. Their rediscovery of the authority of the Word of God led them to reclaim lost truths of great importance. The recovery of such biblical doctrines as justification by grace alone through faith and the priesthood of all believers were recoveries of no small significance. But the reformers did not recover the one thing necessary to the life of the church; namely, the Holy Spirit. A rediscovery of the Holy Spirit in experience and doctrine has been the essential element in the renewal of the church in our time. Its impact upon the church's life in the twentieth century has been compared to the impact of the Reformation upon the Church's doctrine in the sixteenth century.[2]

THE RECOVERY OF THE NEW TESTAMENT EXPERIENCE OF THE HOLY SPIRIT

The twentieth century has witnessed a renewed emphasis upon the Holy Spirit's person and work. But the renewed emphasis upon His person has been stimulated by a fuller recognition of His work. The two are inseparably linked. A theology of the Spirit's person cannot be a matter of personal conviction where the Spirit's person is known only through a baptismal formula, a liturgical benediction, or a creedal statement. We know the Holy Spirit's person through His action, His benefits, through what He is allowed to do for us, in us, and through us. His person cannot be "personally" confessed by us apart from our experience of Him and His power in our lives.

In Scripture the Holy Spirit's person is revealed through the outworking of God's redemptive economy. We do not fully know the Triune God until we know Him as Holy Spirit. Revelation involves the disclosure of God's full person and will. The one God of Scripture wills to make Himself known as Father, Son, and Holy Spirit. This is the order in which we express it theologically. It is really more accurate, however, to say that our experience of God follows the order of Spirit, Son, and Father for our knowledge of the Father and the Son is always through the Holy Spirit. This was Henry Van Dusen's thesis in the book he entitled *Spirit Son and Father* (1958). And it was the point James Dunn was making when he wrote, "Any dogma of the Trinity which does not give pride of place to experience will inevitably be a lifeless abstraction, the worst sort of theological dilettantism." It has been the recovery of the New Testament experience of the Holy Spirit in our time that has brought a renewed emphasis upon the Holy Spirit's divine person. What follows in this chapter is an attempt to outline the movement of experience in Scripture, first within the context of Old Testament monotheism and then in the New Testament.

THE SPIRIT IN HEBREW THOUGHT

"Hear, O Israel: The Lord our God is one Lord. You shall love the Lord your God with all your heart, and with all your soul, and with all your might" (Deuteronomy 6:4, 5; *NKJ*). With this proclamation to the Israelites before they crossed the Jordan river to take possession of the promised land, Moses reminded the delivered people of God's essential unity. This terse summary, known to Jews as the "Shema," from the opening Hebrew verb *shema*, which means "hear," was regarded by Jewish rabbis and by Jesus as the heart of Jewish law (Mark 12:29, 30).

Israel's covenant relation with God centered in the fact that God is One. To this one God the Israelites owed their undivided love and loyalty. Monotheism (the belief that God is one) was central to virtually everything the Hebrews knew about God. He was the sole Creator, the only deliverer they knew in their history. He was the object of undivided love and loyalty for those faithful to the covenant. In Judaism, there could not conceivably be more than one God. Jewish monotheism stood in stark contrast to the polytheism of Israel's pagan neighbors who followed "strange gods," engaged in idol making, and lived with divided loyalties.

The unity of God (that is, the "oneness" of God) was the controlling concept through which the Hebrews understood the "Spirit of God" in the Old Testament. The fuller revelation of God's Tri-unity would have to await New Testament disclosure. In the light of New Testament revelation, we know that the divinity of the Holy Spirit's person was intimated in many ways, but it was never developed in belief or doctrine in the Old Testament.

The Spirit in Hebrew thought was rightly understood to be the Spirit of God. In the New Testament, the same monotheistic emphasis continued (Genesis 1:2; Job 33:4; Matthew 3:16; Romans 8:9). We do well to remember that the New Testament is no less monotheistic in its teaching than the Old Testament. Our thinking about God must always be controlled by monotheism. God is one, and the Holy Spirit cannot be separated from that unity. The extent to which Hebrew prophets protected God's unity can help us better appreciate its biblical emphasis. For example, even when the Spirit was spoken of in the Old Testament as a spirit of judgment, or His work was described as being mischievous in its effects, it was said to proceed from God. In such problematic texts we are not to understand that God is the author of moral evil but that the Spirit always proceeds from God, even when the Spirit's effects are troublesome (Judges 9:23; 1 Samuel 16:14; 16:23; 18:10; 19:9; Isaiah 45:7).

More often, however, the Spirit of God in the Old Testament was associated with those attributes which reveal God's moral perfection. Holiness and righteousness were two such attributes. Hebrew prophets spoke of God as "the Holy One of Israel." God's righteousness was also a prominent theme, particularly of Isaiah who spoke of God as One who is "exalted in righteousness." An understanding of God's holiness and righteousness led the Israelites to understand their own sinfulness and moral impurity. The moral qualities in God, which God required of His covenant people, were not natural moral qualities in the people themselves. Only the "holy" Spirit which proceeded from God could produce the moral ends which God required. The Spirit of God was understood then as a Spirit of righteousness and holiness. The well-known "Psalm of the Spirit" expresses David's dependence upon the gracious God of Israel for moral cleansing through the Spirit. "Have mercy upon me, O God, according to thy lovingkindness: according unto the multitude of thy tender mercies blot out my transgressions. . . . Create in me a clean heart, O God; and renew a right spirit within me. Cast me not away from thy presence; and take not thy holy spirit from me. Restore unto me the joy of thy salvation; and uphold me with thy free spirit" (Psalm 51:1, 10-12). In addition to this Psalm reference, the Spirit is also designated "holy" in Isaiah 63:10, 11 where the prophet speaks of God's graciousness and kindness to Israel in delivering them up out of Egypt, and of God's putting His "holy" Spirit in the midst of them (v. 11). Yet, the people rebelled against God and grieved His "holy" Spirit, Isaiah says (v. 10)

Although the Spirit is not designated "holy" in the Old Testament, except in these instances, the association of the Spirit with God's holy nature and Law is common. The faithful Israelite never doubted that the Spirit which proceeds from God is a Spirit of righteousness and holiness.

The Spirit also represented God's free grace in the Old Testament. What God's holiness and righteousness demanded of the people of God, the Spirit of God provided (Isaiah 28:6; 30:1; Zechariah 12:20). Through His Spirit, God provided all that His purpose required: " 'Not by might, nor by power, but by My Spirit,' Says the Lord of hosts" (Zechariah 4:6, *NKJ).*

From the time of their deliverance out of Egypt, the Israelite nation had been formed and directed by the Spirit of God. Israel was God's covenant people (Isaiah 63:10-14). But they were also a rebellious people. Time and time again the people rebelled against God and broke the covenant. Consequently, the nation was eventually scattered in exile. Still, the prophets foresaw a time when God would restore the nation to life and place His people again in their own land. This too would be accomplished through God's life-giving Spirit. Ezekiel prophesied God's intent, "I will restore the fortunes of Jacob and have mercy upon the whole house of Israel and I will be jealous for my holy name. They shall forget their shame, and all the treachery they have practiced against me, when they dwell securely in their land with none to make them afraid . . . Then they shall know that I am the Lord their God because I sent them into exile among the nations, and then gathered them into their own land. I will leave none of them remaining among the nations any more; and I will not hide my face any more from them, when I pour out my Spirit upon the house of Israel, says the Lord God" (Ezekiel 39:25-29; Isaiah 4:4; 28:6; 32:15).

The Spirit of God was God's Life-Giver. He was Israel's hope for the future. The life-giving Spirit of God was the only hope which Ezekiel foresaw for the valley of dry bones. In his vision of the future, the bones came together and found new life though the Spirit (Ezekiel 37:14). Only the breath of God *(ruach)* could give Israel new life (37:5,6). The nation's hope for the future would be realized only through moral and spiritual renewal by the Spirit.

The Spirit of God was also associated with attributes of God which were nonmoral in character. Omnipresence (the "every-whereness" of God) was such a divine quality. The assurance that the God of Israel was near, even in the midst of the people, was the nation's greatest comfort. Hebrew prophets always maintained the transcendence of Yahweh in their thinking, carefully distinguishing between the infinite Creator and the finite creature. But they never relegated their God to inaccessible regions beyond. Yahweh was exalted, but He was not believed to be remote. The whole of their experiences taught them that God willed to dwell among them. In Eden, God had communed with Adam and Eve before their rebellion. After the Hebrews were delivered from Egypt, the Lord went before the people in a pillar of cloud by day and a pillar of fire by night and "did not depart from before the people" (Exodus 13:21, 22; *RSV).* On Sinai, the Lord descended to reveal His law to the people (Exodus 19:20). At the tent of meeting, the Lord met with Moses and spoke to him "as a man speaks to his friend" (Exodus 33:11, *RSV).* The Ark of the Covenant was a visible reminder of God's presence among the people. It was housed in the sanctuary, a sign that the heavenly Lord was present with His people (Exodus 25:8).

The Lord's presence was experienced and known through His Spirit. God's pervasive presence could be a source of joy and comfort, or it could serve as a reminder that there are no secret sins before an ever-present God. The prayers and psalms of the people besought the God of Israel to come near to them and draw them to Himself through His Spirit: "Renew a right spirit within me; cast me not away from thy presence and take not thy holy Spirit from me," David prayed. In another place, the psalmist asked, "Whither shall I go from thy Spirit? Or whither shall I flee from thy presence? If I ascend to heaven, thou art there! If I make my bed in sheol, thou art there!"

Omnipotence (the "all-powerfulness" of God) was another attribute with which the Spirit was closely associated. Israel knew nothing of a first cause or prime mover in the manner of Greek philosophers. Israel's God was a "living" God who participates and acts within the order He has created. His presence was known to be active through His Spirit. Divine power and life were fundamental concepts underlying the Old Testament meaning of Spirit. The root word for Spirit in Hebrew is *ruach* which has many shades of meaning, but it carries two meanings of singular importance: "wind" and "breath."

Those who lived in the desert environment of the Middle East knew the powerful effects the desert winds could have. These winds shaped and affected everything in their path, even the behavior of men and the elements of nature. In the Old Testament, the Spirit of God *(ruach)* was likened to wind as a form of divine energy.

Samson was moved by divine energy when the Spirit of the Lord rushed upon him and he tore the lion apart (Judges 14:6). In creation, the Spirit of God acted as a creative force when, "By the word of the Lord the heavens were made and all their host by the ruach (breath) of his mouth" (Psalm 103:16). Or, God could renew the "face of the ground" by sending forth His life-giving breath (Psalm 104:30). Whatever God willed to do, in men or in nature, He did through the divine energy of His Spirit.

In the older literature of the Old Testament, the Spirit of God was the recognized source of superhuman strength, courage, skill, judgment, and wisdom. In Numbers, God took part of the leadership burden from Moses and enabled the elders to share it by putting His Spirit upon them (Numbers 11:15). In Judges, the Spirit of the Lord took possession of Gideon, and he sounded the trumpet of war against Israel's enemies (Judges 6:34). The Spirit of the Lord gave Jephthah a great victory over the Ammonites (Judges 11:29). Through the Spirit, the young man Samson was "stirred up" (Judges 13:25), given superhuman strength (Judges 14:6, 19; 15:14), turned into "another man" (1 Samuel 10:6), and made to prophesy (1 Samuel 10:10). When the Spirit of the Lord came upon Saul, his anger was greatly kindled against the enemies of Israel, and he gathered the people together for battle (1 Samuel 11:6). In Exodus, Bezaleel and Aholiab were enabled by the Spirit to do special artistic work required for the tent of meeting and its furnishings (Exodus 31:1-11). All that the purpose of God required, the power of God performed.

It would not be accurate, however, to portray the Spirit as mere force or divine energy. There was always something personal about the Spirit which proceeded from God. A second meaning of ruach was "breath." Breath was more personal than wind because it assumed consciousness, awareness, someone who breathes. Divine life and personality was understood to be the source of human life and personality. The Spirit of God was the point of contact between the Creator and the creature. "God breathed into man's nostrils the breath of life and man became a living creature" (Genesis 2:7). Job acknowledged that, "The Spirit of God has made me, and the breath of the Almighty gives me life" (Job 33:4). And, Job noted, "If God should take back his Spirit to himself, and gather to himself his breath, all flesh would perish together, and man would return to dust" (Job 34:14, 15). The God who creates by His Spirit also preserves His creation through His Spirit. Creation and preservation are works of God's Spirit. The Spirit's person is the very ground of all else in creation that is personal.

Old Testament prophets also saw an inseparable link between God's Spirit and His communicated Word. The Word of God meant more than mere words, the conveyance of meaning through symbols. The Word was itself a veritable cause, a working out of the will of God. What God speaks, the power of the Spirit performs. What God wills is done. Within the Word of God is the power of God to accomplish it (Jeremiah 1:9; Isaiah 55:11; Psalm 33:6, 9).

From the time of the first great prophet Moses, until the last great prophets Haggai, Zechariah, and Malachi, the Lord raised up prophets in Israel, put His words in their mouth, and fulfilled the Word through His Spirit (Zechariah 7:12). What was spoken or written by the inspiration of the Spirit was fulfilled by the power of the Spirit. For that reason, the test of any purported word from God was its fulfillment (Deuteronomy 18:22). Everything that had been inspired by the Spirit was not contained in Scripture, but everything contained in Scripture was believed to be inspired because it had come through the Spirit. The Spirit of God was known as the Spirit of prophecy. Paul wrote to Timothy and advised him that the Old Testament Scriptures were true and profitable because they were "God-breathed" (that is, inspired by the Holy Spirit, 2 Timothy 3:16).

The Spirit of God and the prophetic word were so closely related in Judaism that when the last prophets died, the Jews assumed that the Spirit of God had departed from Israel and would not return until the time of the Messiah. The messianic age was expected to be a time when a great outpouring of the prophetic Spirit would come upon all the people of Israel. Not only upon a few, as in the past, but upon even the servants and handmaidens (Joel 2:28, 29). An outpouring of the Spirit upon the Messiah was expected to be His special equipping for the messianic task. As Isaiah prophesied, "The spirit of the Lord shall rest upon him" (Isaiah 11:2; 61:1). Through the Spirit of God, Israel was expected to become a messianic people.

The Holy Spirit did come upon Jesus at the beginning of His public ministry, and the relation between the Word and the Spirit continued. As Messiah, Jesus fulfilled the offices of Spirit-anointed prophets, priests, and kings. The Spirit of God which descended upon Jesus at the beginning of His public ministry equipped and prepared Him for the fulfillment of these offices (Mark 1:9-12; Hebrews 1:8, 9). All that Jesus revealed about God, and all that He accomplished through His earthly ministry, He did in the power of the Holy Spirit.

THE CONTINUING REVELATION OF THE SPIRIT'S PERSON

There is then a clear and important doctrine of the Holy Spirit in the Old Testament which prepares us for a fuller revelation of the Spirit in the New Testament. It is not the distinctively Christian doctrine of the Spirit. But what is revealed about the Spirit of God in the Old Testament does not misrepresent the truth about the Spirit's person or work. If it is inadequate, it is because of the progressive nature of God's self-disclosure. The fuller revelation of the Spirit's divine person could only be known through the fuller revelation of God's redemptive economy. The Old prepared the way for the New. The understanding we have of the Spirit from the Old Testament enables us to better understand the revelation of His person and work in the New Testament.

Specific truths are taught concerning the Holy Spirit's person which carry over into the New Testament: not least of which is our understanding that a knowledge of the Spirit's person cannot merely be a matter of speculative dogma. The Holy Spirit confronts us as a datum of experience. We really know Him in terms of His actions and His benefits. The Spirit of God is God active.

The Spirit's person in the Old Testament is not definitively distinguished from Jehovah God because they are One. The unity of their persons and the interrelatedness of their work is essential to our understanding of God's nature. In the Old Testament, the emphasis is always upon God's unity. The Spirit is always the "Spirit of God" or the "Spirit of the Lord."

A monotheistic emphasis is equally true in the New Testament. Paul speaks of the Holy Spirit as "the Spirit of Jesus" and "the Spirit of Christ" (Philippians 1:19; Galatians 4:6). The "Spirit of God" and the "Spirit of Christ" can hardly be separated from the "Holy Spirit" because God is one. Just as the work of the Spirit is interpenetrated by the work of the Father and Son, their divine person must be understood in terms of Trinity in Unity (Acts 16:6, 7; Romans 8:9).

We know the character of the Spirit's person through

His divine action. The Holy Spirit reveals God's free grace and moral character. Through the activity of the Holy Spirit, the presence and power of God are manifested. The Spirit of God who moved upon the face of the waters is seen to be the source of extraordinary power, wisdom, skill, and divine revelation. His "breath" is the life of men. When God blows His breath (Spirit) and men are inspired, they become instruments of the divine Word. When that breath is gone, men die (literally "expire" or "breathe out"). The Spirit gives and sustains life. God's living presence is mediated through Him. His presence is "holy" because He is Holy Spirit. He is the "Holy One of Israel," the righteous God.

THE PERSON AND WORK OF THE HOLY SPIRIT IN THE NEW TESTAMENT

Old Testament prophets expected there to be an unusual revelation of God's Spirit in the messianic age (Isaiah 44:1-5; Ezekiel 37:1-14; 47:1-12; Joel 2:28-32). The coming of the Messiah would be accompanied by the Spirit. He would be the sign of the New Age.

The link between Jesus and the Holy Spirit is seen as Jesus' person and work are revealed in the power of the Spirit. The Spirit is seen in virtually every aspect of Jesus' ministry. His miraculous conception in Mary is by the Holy Spirit (Matthew 1:18, 20; Luke 1:35). Simeon is inspired by the Holy Spirit to bless the baby Jesus in the Temple (Luke 2:27). At His baptism, the Spirit comes upon Jesus (Matthew 3:16; Mark 1:10; Luke 3:22). Immediately afterwards, the Spirit drives Jesus into the wilderness to be tempted in preparation for His ministry (Mark 1:12; Matthew 4:1; Luke 4:1). Following His temptation, Jesus returns to Galilee "full of the Spirit" where His ministry begins in the power of the Holy Spirit (Luke 4:1). The power of the Spirit is particularly evident in Jesus' casting out of unclean spirits. Against those who would attribute the power of the Holy Spirit to unclean spirits, Jesus sternly warns of the danger of blaspheming the Holy Spirit (Matthew 12:28-32; Mark 3:29; Luke 12:10). To reject the power of the Holy Spirit, and attribute His power to evil, is tantamount to rejecting the power of the New Age and the forgiveness Jesus offers through the Holy Spirit. Whoever rejects the Spirit through whom God wills to offer forgiveness, can only expect to encounter Him as a judge. He who refuses to be won by the Holy Spirit cannot be won at all.

This is in fulfillment of what Isaiah prophesied concerning the Messiah, upon whom the Lord promised to put His Spirit. Through the Spirit-filled Messiah, judgment would come to the Gentiles. Matthew declared: "Behold my servant, whom I have chosen; my beloved, in whom my soul is well pleased: I will put my Spirit upon him, and he shall show judgment to the Gentiles" (Isaiah 42:1-4; Matthew 12:18). Jesus' announcement of the kingdom and reign of God is a message both of hope and judgment. God's kingdom breaks in with salvation and hope for the penitent and trusting. But it becomes a judgment upon those who ignore its reality and seek to circumvent its provision. Ananias and Sapphira are an example of those who deny the reality of the messianic age and encounter God's judgment.

The Age of the Spirit is an age when unusual things happen in the community of Spirit-filled believers. What happened in Acts is an example of what can happen in such a community. Yet, despite the extraordinary acts of the Spirit, His work was never separated from the historical Jesus or the life of the church. As Hendrikus Berkhof points out, it has always been the nature of the Holy Spirit to hide Himself in Christ and the operations of the church.[3] The Holy Spirit never ceases to be the "Spirit of Christ" whose work is done in the community of believers.

The eschatological link between Jesus and the Holy Spirit is also seen in the manner in which believers experience the inward reality of the New Age. Paul speaks of the Holy Spirit as a foretaste, as a first installment of the Christian's redemption. The Spirit is God's link between time and eternity, old time and redeemed time, the old and new creation (1 Corinthians 2:9, 10; 2 Corinthians 5:5; Romans 8:11, 23). The Spirit is the glory and power of the New Age inaugurated by Christ (1 Peter 1:5; 4:14). Those who belong to the life of the New Age, who have "tasted . . . the powers of the age to come" (Hebrews 6:5, *NKJ*), are partakers of the Holy Spirit (Hebrews 1:2). "Walking according to the Spirit" is the Christian's norm for living in the New Age (2 Corinthians 5:17; Galatians 5:16-18, 25).

Paul uses a variety of expressions that indicate the inseparable relation between Christ and the Spirit. Throughout his writings, he interchangeably refers to the Spirit, the Spirit of Christ, the Spirit of the Lord, the Spirit of Jesus, the Spirit of Him who raised Jesus, of being in Christ, being in the Spirit, having Christ in you, and having the Spirit. He speaks of the Spirit as God's power through whom sin is overcome in our flesh (Romans 8:1-5; 10-13). The Spirit is God's presence in us now, God's pledge or guarantee of complete redemption (2 Corinthians 1:22; 5:5). In some places, Paul virtually identifies the Spirit with Christ (2 Corinthians 3:17; Romans 3:26, 34). Just as the Holy Spirit is the "Spirit of God" in the Old Testament, He is the "Spirit of Christ" in the New Testament.

The Scriptures clearly teach that the Holy Spirit is a divine person (Acts 16:16; John 14:16; 2 Corinthians 13:14; Matthew 28:19; Ephesians 4:30), but they do so without separating the Spirit's person from the unity of the Godhead. The disclosure of God's Triune essence necessitates the revelation of the Spirit's person as it does the Father's and the Son's. God wills to reveal His full person as Father, Son and Holy Spirit.

Some have argued that belief in the Son is also belief in the Holy Spirit, that their close relation means that one need not have a distinctive knowledge of the Holy Spirit. Such reasoning, however, is erroneous. According to this logic there would not even be any need for a definite acceptance of the Son because belief in the Father would also be a belief in the Son. In emphasizing the oneness of the Godhead we must not lose sight of God's trinitarian nature. God has willed that in His redemptive economy His Triune person should be revealed and received. In Scripture and through experience God allows us to know the divine person of the Holy Spirit just as He allows us to know the person of the Father and the Son.

CREEDAL STATEMENTS ABOUT THE HOLY SPIRIT

In a document addressed to the bishops of the west, one year after the Council of Constantinople in 381, the full divinity of the Holy Spirit was officially affirmed by a church synod for the first time. In the Nicene confession (A.D. 325) relatively little had been said about the Holy Spirit. In the Niceno-Constantinopolitan Creed, which resulted from the Second Ecumenical Council in 381, more was said about the Holy Spirit. But there was no specific assertion that the Holy Spirit is a divine person, equal to the Father and Son. It was not until A.D. 382 that the Christian church officially affirmed the Spirit's divinity in creedal form. When it did, the document read:

> According to this faith there is one Godhead, Power and Substance of the Father and of the Son and of the Holy Ghost; the dignity being equal, and the majesty being equal in three perfect essences [hypostaseis] and three perfect persons.[4]

Toward the close of the sixth century, the so-called "filioque" clause (which means literally "and from the Son") was added to the earlier form of the Niceno-Constantinopolitan creed by the western part of Christendom. This clause was added at the Council of Toledo in A.D. 589. It read: "And [I believe] in the Holy Ghost, the Lord and Giver of Life, who proceeds from the Father and from the Son." The primary interest in the filioque clause was, no doubt, to emphasize the coequality of the Son with the Father, the issue that had been debated for five centuries during the Trinitarian controversy. The use of the filioque clause, however, offended the theologians of the Greek church who protested that the doctrine could not be found in Scripture and that the creed was not made by an Ecumenical Council (see John 15:26). The controversy ultimately led to a schism between the eastern and western branches of Christendom in the 11th century.

The intellectual controversy that surrounded the debate about the Holy Spirit's person illustrates that the Spirit's person can only be truly affirmed where the objective and subjective elements in Christian revelation are balanced. The need for such balance is best illustrated through the proper use of creedal statements about the Holy Spirit.

A creed (from the Latin *credo* meaning "I believe") is a statement of confession about one's belief and faith. The earliest creeds are in the Bible itself. When Jesus asked His disciples, "Whom say ye that I am?" Peter replied, "You are the Christ, the Son of the living God." Peter's answer represented a personal confession of faith, inspired by the Holy Spirit. When Thomas confessed Jesus as "Lord and God" after seeing Jesus' wounded side and nail-scarred hands, he too was affirming a personal faith.

Creeds have been very important in the history of the Christian church. The church has always been involved in communicating the faith, in handing down the deposit of faith from one generation to another. Creeds facilitate that process of transmission. They reflect the shape, the form, that faith has taken in the Christian tradition. Creeds have served valuable functions in combating heresy, as public statements of faith, and personal confessions in Christian worship.

Some Christians have denounced creeds altogether, largely out of a deference for "spontaneity" and "presentism" over form and tradition. This attitude is unfortunate because it assumes that creeds are empty and formal, which is not necessarily the case. They do not have to be empty and meaningless, the mere repetition of archaic theological formulas. Creeds can be both fresh and personal expressions of faith.

Christians need an objective statement about their faith in God. An acknowledgement of the Holy Spirit's divinity is just as essential as an acknowledgement of the divinity of the Father and the Son. The Church has an authoritative deposit of truth in Scripture from which to make its confession. Scripture is the final norm for all Christian doctrine, including the doctrine of the Spirit's person. Experience that is authentically Christian must rest upon what is given as divine revelation. All creeds and dogma must be judged by the authority of the Word.

This does not mean, however, that Christians can surrender the subjective aspect of revelation. While God is not known *as* human experience, God is known *in* human experience.[5] This is how God has willed to make His revelation complete. A revelation objectively given cannot be totally separated from revelation subjectively received from the Holy Spirit. The divinity of the Holy Spirit is known from Scripture. But the church does not know the Spirit's divinity simply because there are proof-texts to which it can point. The Spirit's divinity is made known through His self-revealing in human experience. The Christian faith is a personal activity. It cannot be inherited. Nor can it be passed along in a mere objective or creedal form.

To know God's person fully is to know God as Father, Son, and Holy Spirit. God's essence is Triune. His Triune essence gives rise to the divine economy in which God is made known in human experience as a Triune Being. Through the Holy Spirit, God enables us to experience Him as Father, as One who creates and nurtures. The Father God makes Himself known in experience as the personal referent of all existence, the ground of all being. God the Son is revealed in God's economy as the One in whom God is enfleshed and made accessible to us. Through the Holy Spirit, we experience the Son in adoption. "Sonship" is our experience of adoption, of belonging to the benevolent Father and His household. Christ's relationship in the household is our model for sonship—He is the "firstborn." We participate in the household and receive its benefits through our relationship to Jesus Christ, in whom we have been adopted. The meaning of our lives is defined by His. His story becomes our story as we identify with Him in death and resurrection and take up the ministry of reconciliation.

Knowing God as Holy Spirit means that we participate in the life of the Spirit and in the revealing of God's redemptive economy in which the Holy Spirit is so vitally involved. As divine person, the Holy Spirit confronts us as "thou," as One with intentionality and will. As divine person, the Spirit engenders purpose in us as He did the early church when he guided the church in its missionary activity (Acts 16:6). His personal agency is made known when we experience Him as Comforter and Advocate (John 14:16). We express our experience of His communion when we pray the liturgical benediction (2 Corinthians 13:14). We acknowledge the fact of His divine authority when we are baptized in His name (Matthew 28:19).

In His sovereign freedom, the Holy Spirit enables us to experience His dynamism in strange ways. He is the power of the New Age, the One whose power bursts forth in miracles, ecstasy, other tongues, spiritual gifts. He is the power and presence of the "living" God who defies all human attempts to rationalize and domesticate His power.

After the Holy Spirit was poured out at Pentecost, the Church so experienced the life and action of the Spirit that some expositors suggest Acts should be called the "Acts of the Holy Spirit." The apostolic church never had any hesitancy in affirming the full divinity of the Holy Spirit. They knew the Spirit to be divine, as they did the Father and Son, because they had experienced His person and power. Our confession of the Holy Spirit's divinity can only be as fresh and meaningful today as our experience of Him. If we are to know the completeness of the Triune God, we must know Him in human experience as He has willed to reveal His person as Holy Spirit. Creedal statements about Him are well and good, but the truth about Him will only be as fresh and as operational as our knowledge of Him.

FOOTNOTES

[1]Christ's relation to God and to man was explored between the Council of Nicaea in A.D. 325 and the Council of Chalcedon in A.D. 451. Most of the discussion centered around the question of the two natures of Christ, the human and the divine. The Christian church affirmed both the full divinity and the full humanity of Jesus Christ. Pentecostals do the same. If there is a weakness in Pentecostal Christology, it

probably lies in the failure of many Pentecostals to take Jesus' full humanity seriously enough. This failure is more often seen in applied rather than textbook theology.

[2]See, for example, two articles by a leading liberal theologian and churchman, Henry Pitt van Dusen, "The Third Force in Christendom," *Life* 44 (June 9, 1958) and "Caribbean Holiday," *Christian Century*, 72 (August 17, 1955). Other leading theologians and churchmen from various denominations have made similar observations.

[3]Hendrikus Berkhof, *The Doctrine of the Holy Spirit* (Richmond, Virginia: Knox, 1964), p. 10.

[4]Cited by Bernard Lohse, *A Short History of Christian Doctrine*, trans. F. Ernest Stoeffler (Philadelphia: Fortress Press, 1980), p. 65.

[5]See R. P. C. Hanson, "The Divinity of the Holy Spirit," *New Theology* no. 7, ed. Martin E. Marty, Dean G. Peerman (New York: Macmillan, 1971), p. 193.

Chapter 4

Baptism in the Holy Spirit

Toward a Definition

The basic theological distinctive of Pentecostalism is the doctrine of the "Baptism in the Holy Spirit." The experience of Spirit-baptism refers to a decisive encounter of the Christian believer with God in which the believer receives a special empowerment of the Holy Spirit for Christian witness and service. Pentecostals believe and teach that the initial evidence of this experience is speaking with other tongues as the Spirit gives the utterance in accordance with Acts 2:4.

In general Christian usage, "Pentecost" is simply a shorthand way of referring to the initial outpouring of the Holy Spirit on the disciples of Jesus as described in Acts chapter 2. The term "Pentecostal" refers to one who has received the experience of Spirit-baptism. "Pentecostalism" refers to a historic movement, dating from the turn of the twentieth century, which arose out of the Holiness Movement in America. The distinguishing mark of the Pentecostal movement was its emphasis upon the Baptism in the Holy Spirit as a "third blessing" or work of grace which was understood to be subsequent to the new birth and cleansing (sanctification). Not all traditional Pentecostals, however, were in agreement about sanctification. Some regarded sanctification as a gradual process rather than an instantaneous work.[1] Consequently, for them, speaking in tongues was the sign of a second rather than a third blessing. Virtually all Pentecostals have, on the other hand, believed in divine healing and the operation of the gifts of the Spirit in the church today. Consequently, these emphases have also been distinguishing marks of classical Pentecostalism.

"Neo-Pentecostalism" is a more recent term that refers to the phenomenon of Pentecostal experience within the historic churches. The movement first received national publicity in the late 1950s when a Presbyterian minister and an Episcopalian congregation reported that they had experienced the Holy Spirit with the evidence of tongues. With added momentum from the Full Gospel Businessmen's Fellowship, itinerants of the Blessed Trinity Society, and the influence of public figures like Oral Roberts, David du Plessis, and David Wilkerson, the movement penetrated deeper into the historic Protestant churches during the decade of the 60s. During the mid 60s a Charismatic revival began among Roman Catholics. First Duquesne University, then at Notre Dame and Michigan State, the experience of Spirit-baptism quickly spread across the country.[2] At present, there is hardly a major denomination in America that has not been penetrated and deeply influenced by the Pentecostal experience. In some cases the extraordinary gifts of the Spirit are now stressed more among neo-Pentecostals than traditional Pentecostals. Ironically enough, the lackluster spiritual life of the historic denominations at the turn of the century which helped give rise to the Pentecostal movement has, in our own day, contributed to the rise of neo-Pentecostalism within the structures of these same churches. What distinguishes the neo-Pentecostalism from traditional Pentecostalism is its lay orientation, its impact upon Christians in higher socioeconomic groups, and the willingness of Spirit-baptized believers in the traditional denominations to retain their doctrinal commitments and remain within the structures of the historic churches.[3]

In light of these developments, it is little wonder that people are again asking what was asked on the Day of Pentecost: "What meaneth this?" What follows is an attempt to answer that question from a Pentecostal perspective, to explain and clarify what traditional Pentecostals believe and teach concerning the Baptism in the Holy Spirit.

THE TEACHING OF SPIRIT-BAPTISM IN CHURCH TRADITION

The Protestant principle of *sola scriptura* means that the Scriptures ought always to be our norm and source of authority for theology. But this principle does not exclude the importance of the light that the tradition of the church oftentimes sheds upon our inquiry into doctrine. One is reminded of John Wesley's statement that something must be wrong with our exegesis if experience and tradition contradict it.[4] One simply cannot ignore 2,000 years of church tradition in his interpretation of the New Testament. A cross-examination of the past is absolutely essential to responsible theological work.

The Pentecostal has no reason to fear the past. He knows that many have been misguided by past traditions, but the knowledgeable Pentecostal also knows that a study of tradition can provide some clarification, even confirmation, of his own faith perspective. The study of history may, of course, serve as a critical check against one's own past as well. One should always bear in mind that unexamined history operates as fate.

An examination of the past has particular importance for the Pentecostal because the doctrine by which he is distinctively identified, the doctrine of the Baptism in the Holy Spirit, has too often been dismissed as some kind of current theological aberration. It is important for the Pentecostal to establish the fact that down through the centuries there has always been a strain of church teaching which held that there is a special distinctive operation or gift of the Holy Spirit that is subsequent to conversion which is referred to in the New Testament as being "baptized in the Holy Spirit."

THE ROMAN CATHOLIC TRADITION

Pentecostal believers have serious differences with the sacramental theology of Roman Catholicism. They disagree with the Catholic understanding of the church, the papacy, mariology, purgatory, and a number of other dogmas that other Protestants have traditionally rejected. But there is at least one important area of agreement in which Pentecostals have been closer to Roman Catholics than they have to mainline Protestants; namely, in their emphasis upon a work of the Holy Spirit in the life of the Christian which is subsequent to the new birth.

A distinction was drawn early in the Roman Catholic tradition between the work of the Spirit whereby one is converted and becomes a Christian and a subsequent work of the Spirit whereby one receives the fullness of the Spirit according to the pattern of Acts 2:4. This distinction was made in the Catholic sacraments of baptism and confirmation where salvation was presented in two stages. To be sure, the Catholic understanding of baptismal grace was in objectivistic and sacramental terms. It was not an evangelical understanding of conversion. Neither do Pentecostals consider confirmation to be an acceptable substitute for the experience of being baptized in the Holy Spirit. But this is not the point. The fact that we are interested in establishing is that early church tradition recognized and allowed for two definitive works of grace wrought through the Holy Spirit.

William J. O'Shea of the Catholic University of America explains the Catholic understanding of these two separate, yet related, works of the Spirit in the following quote from his *Sacraments of Initiation:*

> In the life of Christ there were two 'anointings' by the Spirit. The first was at the moment of the incarnation; that one established him as the Son of God . . . By this anointing which is the hypostatic union Jesus was constituted king and priest at the same time. It was his royal and priestly consecration.
>
> The other anointing took place when he was

baptized in the Jordan. At that moment he accepted his mission as 'suffering servant' and messiah-redeemer. He was anointed then as the great agent of the divine plan of salvation. This was his prophetical anointing.

These two separate, yet related, anointings must be reproduced in the life of the Christian. The first anointing of the Spirit takes place at baptism, making him the adopted son of God. The second takes place at confirmation when the Spirit descends upon him again to make him a prophet, to equip him with the gifts he needs to enable him to live fully the life of an adopted son, and to fulfill his mission in the Church. . . .

Jesus was anointed with the Spirit at the time of his baptism, but it was at Pentecost that the apostles were anointed by the Spirit. The Spirit we receive in confirmation is the Spirit of Pentecost. . . .[5]

What is significant in this two-stage operation of the Spirit, from the Pentecostal's point of view, is its admission that there is biblical precedence for a special work of the Holy Spirit that completes and perfects the Spirit's work in regeneration and that this work had its genesis at Pentecost.[6] Catholics see this second work of the Spirit in connection with a special anointing for witness and service, but the Catholic doctrine of confirmation also has as its aim to conform the believer to Christ, to reproduce Christ in him.[7] Like the Wesleyan doctrine of entire sanctification, the Catholic doctrine of confirmation prescribes an experience of the Spirit that is subsequent to regeneration. Neither the Catholics nor the Wesleyans regard this experience as unrelated to regeneration. Both understand it to be a moral completion or perfection of "character" already begun in regeneration.

DOCTRINAL DEVELOPMENTS WITHIN PROTESTANTISM

In the sixteenth century the Protestant reformers rejected the Catholic sacrament of confirmation, and all emphasis upon a definitive work of the Spirit subsequent to regeneration disappeared for a while. Calvin labeled the Catholic teaching of confirmation "horrible blasphemies" and totally rejected the Catholic exegesis of Scriptures that supported the view of a work of grace subsequent to the new birth that completes what has been begun in regeneration (for example, Acts 8:14-17; 19:1,2).[8] In the seventeenth century a renewed emphasis upon a second and subsequent work of the Spirit emerged again in the form of the Puritan experience of assurance, but it was not until the eighteenth century that the two-stage perspective was again raised to doctrinal status—this time by John Wesley.[9]

Wesley's emphasis upon entire sanctification is well known. It was the distinct doctrine that he bequeathed to Methodism. The experience of holiness (entire sanctification) or perfection in love was, in the thinking of Wesley, a divine gift subsequent to justification. This second work of grace was not believed to be unrelated to the Spirit's work in regeneration but was understood to be the completion of that which regeneration anticipates; namely, a holy life.

There were striking similarities between the Wesleyan doctrine of entire sanctification and the Roman Catholic doctrine of confirmation. Unlike the Reformers, both acknowledged a definitive work of the Holy Spirit subsequent to conversion. Scholars in both traditions cited the same passages in the Book of Acts to distinguish the fullness of the Spirit from the birth of the Spirit. And both associated the fullness of the Spirit with the completion or perfection of character begun in regeneration.[10]

Neither tradition, however, associated this second work of the Spirit with Spirit-baptism, with what the Holiness Movement would later call "Baptism in the Holy Spirit." The church had not traditionally distinguished in terminology between water-baptism and Spirit-baptism. It was the Holiness Movement in the nineteenth century that brought Spirit-baptism into prominence as a distinct doctrine. The "Higher Life" teaching in British Holiness circles emphasized a distinction between justification by faith through which one is delivered from the penalty of sin and a second divine work of sanctification through which one is delivered from the power of sin.[11] This second work of the Spirit was called "the baptism of the Holy Ghost," but speaking in tongues was not viewed as the evidence of it. In the Holiness Movement the experience of Spirit-baptism was associated both with cleansing and sanctification and with empowerment for witness and service.[12]

In America the phrase "baptism in the Holy Spirit" was seemingly first used at Oberlin College by Asa Mahan and Charles Finney in connection with Oberlin perfectionism. After the Civil War the shift from the language of Christian perfectionism to Baptism of the Holy Spirit ocurred rapidly. The language of Pentecost could be found everywhere. Everything from camp meetings to choirs were being described as "Pentecostal." There were "Pentecostal sermons," "Pentecostal testimonies," and "Pentecostal churches."[13] Prominent Holiness churches carried the name "Pentecostal" as part of their official name. The Church of the Nazarene was originally called the Pentecostal Church of the Nazarene; in Scotland the Nazarene congregations called themselves the Pentecostal Church of Scotland.

Other factors were at work in the last quarter of the nineteenth century which became an important part of Pentecostal experience and doctrine after Azusa Street in 1906. Holiness leaders had already aroused new interest in spiritual gifts by teaching that they should still operate in the Church. Interest was particularly strong on divine healing.[14] Toward the close of the century R. A. Torrey helped shift the emphasis away from the holiness teaching that the Baptism with the Holy Spirit is for the purpose of cleansing from sin to an emphasis upon witness and service (based principally on Luke 24:49, Acts 1:5, 8).[15] When the outpouring of the Holy Spirit occurred in Tennessee/North Carolina, Kansas, and California, at the turn of the twentieth century, the forces which gave rise to the Pentecostal Movement were already in motion.

THE PENTECOSTAL DISTINCTIVE

The one teaching that did not precede the Pentecostal movement was that tongues is the initial evidence of being baptized in the Holy Ghost. The Pentecostal outpouring had been accompanied by the strange phenomena of speaking in tongues. When the recipients turned to the Scriptures for an explanation they discovered that the same phenomena had accompanied Spirit-baptism in Acts. Based upon what they discovered from the pattern in Acts, Pentecostals concluded that speaking in tongues must be the initial physical evidence of a person's having received the Baptism in the Holy Spirit.

This decision, more than any other, gave theological distinctiveness to the Pentecostal Movement of the twentieth century. Those Pentecostals who came out of the Holiness tradition could only interpret their experience to represent a third crisis experience (regeneration, sanctification, and baptism in the Holy Spirit), the latter being evidenced by speaking in other tongues as the Spirit gave the utterance. It would be difficult to conceive of the rise of modern Pentecostalism without the background of the Wesleyan doctrine of "Christian Perfection" and its nineteenth century transmutation into the doctrine of "Pentecostal sanctification."[16] This can be attested by the fact that virtually all of the early Pentecostal bodies stressed three crisis experiences. The Holiness Movement had provided the underlying theological framework for Pentecostalism. The exceptions, of course, were those Pentecostals with a more reformed theology who taught two crises (conversion and a "baptism of the Spirit" for the empowering for service evidenced by speaking in tongues—combined with a more gradual doctrine of sanctification).[17] To those who remained within the Holiness tradition, the new form of Pentecostalism could only appear to be a "holiness heresy." This feeling was exemplified by the Nazarenes who promptly dropped the word "Pentecostal" from their official church name lest they be identified with the emerging Pentecostal movement and their doctrine of tongues.[18] Those from mainline Reformation churches viewed Pentecostals with even more suspicion for they saw no need for any definitive work of the Spirit subsequent to regeneration. It was only after the Pentecostal movement had taken on worldwide significance and had begun to impact their own churches that Catholics and mainline Protestants alike began to take a new look at Pentecostals and reexamine their theology.

WHAT PENTECOSTALS TEACH ABOUT THE BAPTISM IN THE HOLY SPIRIT

All Pentecostals obviously do not believe and teach exactly the same thing about the Holy Spirit. It would be unrealistic to expect that.[19] But there does seem to be a common body of teaching concerning Spirit-baptism with which most Pentecostals are in essential agreement. It is this common belief to which we will now turn our attention. For if Pentecostal theology is to be judged, it ought to be judged by what the movement publicly teaches about Spirit-baptism. The first tenet to which all Pentecostals will subscribe is the belief that:

A. Spirit-baptism is a biblically based experience.

Part of the difficulty that non-Pentecostals have with the Pentecostal teaching about the Baptism in the Holy Spirit stems from the fact that the noun form of the phrase "Baptism in the Holy Spirit" does not occur in the New Testament. Pentecostals are aware of this, just as they are aware that such terms as "trinity," "rapture," and "atonement" are not New Testament terms either. Yet these are important terms for us today because they aptly describe realities which are clearly taught in Scripture. The test of a doctrine does not rest entirely upon an exact duplication of language. The real test of a doctrine lies in its correspondence with the clear teaching of Scripture.

The verb "baptize" is used a number of times in connection with the Holy Spirit (Matthew 3:11; Mark 1:8; Luke 3:16; John 1:33; Acts 1:5; 11:16). All of these references relate to the expectation of John the Baptist that Jesus would baptize with the Holy Spirit. Thus, it is fitting to begin a New Testament study of Spirit-baptism with John's prophecy. The expectation that

Jesus would baptize in the Holy Spirit was obviously well known because every gospel writer referred to it. It is the only prophecy of John that appears in all four gospel traditions. "I indeed baptize you with water unto repentance," John said, "but . . . he [Jesus] shall baptize you with the Holy Ghost, and with fire." After the 120 were filled with the Holy Ghost on the Day of Pentecost and spoke in tongues the church knew that it had received the baptism of the Spirit which John had promised. This is made clear in Acts 11:16 where Peter declared, after the Holy Spirit has been poured out upon Cornelius and his household, "Then I remembered the word of the Lord, how He said, 'John indeed baptized with water, but you shall be baptized with the Holy Spirit' " (NKJ). The absence of the noun form "Baptism in the Holy Spirit" is no cause for concern. For there can be no serious doubt that an act of being baptized (verb) in the Spirit inevitably results in a Baptism (noun) in the Spirit.

Spirit-baptism in the New Testament was more than a doctrine. As Edward Schweizer notes, "Long before the Spirit was an article of doctrine it was a fact in the experience of the primitive Church."[20] Leslie Newbigin once commented that most Christians today would not likely be asked the same question that the apostle asked the converts of Apollos in Acts 19:2: "Did you receive the Holy Spirit when you believed?" Modern successors would be more likely to ask, "Did you believe exactly what we teach?" Or, "Were the hands that were laid on you our hands?"[21] The reason for such questions being that since the first century Spirit-baptism has been identified primarily with ritual acts (baptism, confirmation) or with a profession of faith in which the gift of the Spirit was believed to be bestowed in connection with the act of faith. Outside Pentecostal and Charismatic bodies, the great majority of Christians in mainline churches today would feel threatened by religious experiences such as we read about in Acts. Most have, in fact, been conditioned by the teachers of the church to be suspicious of religious experience. This has been particularly true of Spirit-baptism. As late as 1950, A. R.

Vidler wrote: "Conscious experience of the presence and life of the Spirit among contemporary Christians is so thin and weak and hampered that conditions do not exist in which one can write with full-blooded conviction on the subject."[22]

One of the reasons why Pentecostals have demonstrated a full-blooded conviction about Spirit-baptism is that they know the reality of this biblical truth through experience. It is more than a teaching, a tradition, or a ritual act administered by an ecclesiastical institution. Spirit-baptism is an "experience," a direct contact with the power and presence of God. It would not be an overstatement to say that Spirit-baptism is never given in such a way that it cannot be experienced. Pentecostals have refocused attention on Spirit-baptism in terms of experience, not for the purpose of exalting experience above everything else, but in the interest of presenting the doctrine in a manner that is consistent both with human experience and the clear teaching of Scripture.[23]

B. Spirit-baptism is a promised gift.

As already noted, all four gospel writers record the prophecy of John the Baptist that Jesus would baptize in the Holy Spirit. In the Gospel of John, at the Feast of Tabernacles, Jesus himself promises that the Spirit will be given to those who believe upon Him and thirst for (that is, desire) the water that He shall give.

"If anyone thirst, let him come to me and drink. He who believes in me as the Scripture has said, 'Out of his heart shall flow rivers of living water.' Now this he said about the Spirit, which those who believed in him were to receive; for as yet the Spirit had not been given, because Jesus was not yet glorified" (John 7:37-39).

At a later occasion when Jesus commissioned His disciples He again reminded them of the promise of the Holy Spirit and commanded them to stay in Jerusalem until they had received the power of the Holy Spirit: "And behold, I send the promise of my father upon you; but stay in the city, until you are clothed with power from on high" (Luke 24:49). Before His ascension Jesus again promised the Spirit and stated the Spirit's purpose:

"But you shall receive power when the Holy Spirit has come upon you; and you shall be my witnesses in Jerusalem and in all Judea and Samaria and to the end of the earth" (Acts 1:8).

In his sermon at Pentecost the Apostle Peter stressed to his hearers that they had received the promised gift from the Father (Acts 2:33); and, that this promised gift was available even to their children and all who were far off (Acts 2:39). Paul's references to the Holy Spirit in Galatians and Ephesians also emphasize the element of promise, connecting the promise of the Spirit with the promise of faith through Abraham. The Holy Spirit, Paul says, has sealed that which was promised and is an advance installment (promise) of that which God still has in store for Christians (2 Corinthians 5:5; 1:22; Romans 8:16, 17, 23: Ephesians 1:13, 14). In Old Testament times the Holy Spirit was the Promised sign of the New Age. In the New Testament the Spirit is the recognized sign that the New Age has come.

The Holy Spirit was poured out at Pentecost then because He had been promised. The church did not receive the Spirit because of anything it did but because God had promised the Spirit and the church was open and receptive to that promise. It was God's will for the Holy Spirit to be poured out upon the church, but God did not force the Holy Spirit upon the church. The Holy Spirit was a promised gift; still, the church had to be receptive. Evil spirits may seek to impose themselves upon the unwary but not the Spirit of God. He never dwells in a temple where He is not welcome.

Scholars from mainline Reformation traditions are often critical of the Pentecostal assertion that there are "conditions" attached to the reception of the Holy Spirit. Following the Reformation emphasis upon grace, theologians like Frederick Bruner accuse Pentecostals of "works righteousness" because they establish conditions for receiving the promised gift of the Holy Spirit. Bruner is typical of the Reformed attitude toward Spirit-baptism in that he equates Spirit-baptism with water baptism, thus stressing the objective nature of faith; emphasizes the passivity of the person receiving the grace of faith, thus seeing all "conditions" as a peril to the doctrine of grace alone; adheres to the Lutheran concept of simultaneously being saint and sinner.[24]

By harping loud and long on the one string of *sola fides* Bruner tries to caricature the Pentecostal position as one oriented toward "works" and blind to the fact that Spirit-baptism is a promised gift. Bruner's work in *A Theology of the Holy Spirit* is scholarly and well documented, and he says many things to which Pentecostals ought to listen, but the work is flawed in its insistence that grace entails passivity on our part. Pentecostals are proud to be part of a tradition that teaches a gospel of grace. But Pentecostals do not interpret grace to mean that God will work His will in people's lives in spite of their closed and calloused hearts. The fact that the Holy Spirit is a promised gift does not mean that there are no conditions whatsoever to one's receiving the gift. None of us fully understand the intricate relation between the working of God's free grace and man's free will, but the comments of J. Rodman Williams on the issue of "conditions" seem particularly relevant:

> There exists a beautiful harmony between God's free action in the Spirit and our openness to it. The Spirit is a gift and therefore cannot be bought; consequently, there is no earning of the Spirit by any amount of prayers, vigils, and the like. The Spirit moves freely and cannot be compelled or coerced by any human contrivance—no matter how astutely performed. But for the very reason that the Spirit acts graciously in freedom, He will not grant a gift where it is not wanted or asked for, nor will He break through barriers that resist His coming. Thus only the open and expectant, the eager and hungry, the askers and seekers (not because of what they do but because of their readiness) receive God's blessing.[25]

Self-surrender is still the condition for the reception of the Spirit. The Spirit can and will move freely and graciously where He finds no resistance. Pride, in all of its subtle forms, is still the chief obstacle in our quest for the spiritual life. The Pentecostal jargon of "giving up" and "letting go" is still important in what it signifies; namely, the necessity of human readiness and cooperation with the Holy Spirit. The Holy Spirit is God's promised gift to the believer, but promise does not imply human passivity nor divine determination apart from our willingness and desire to receive God's gift. As Karl Barth put it, "Only where the Spirit is sighed, cried, and prayed for does he become present and newly active."[26]

C. Spirit-baptism is not Regeneration.

The most distinctive Pentecostal doctrine, and the one which separates it most clearly from mainline Protestant bodies, is the distinction which Pentecostals make between regeneration and Spirit-baptism. Contrary to those who teach that Spirit-baptism means conversion, regardless of whether they view conversion as synonymous with water-baptism or as a personal profession of faith, Pentecostals believe that the Baptism in the Holy Spirit is an experience distinct from and subsequent to conversion. The doctrine of subsequence, Pentecostals believe, is based upon the clear teaching of Scripture:

It is erroneous to conclude that the apostles were not saved men until they received the baptism of the Holy Spirit at Pentecost. The Scriptures clearly teach that they were already regenerate men although they were not yet baptized with the Holy Ghost. Jesus' disciples were not yet equipped for their vocation, but Jesus himself indicated that they were redemptively united to Him prior to Pentecost. Who could doubt that the disciples were converted before Pentecost when Jesus clearly said that they had received His Word and kept it (John 17:8)? Unconverted men do not receive the Word of God and keep it. Jesus also indicated that the disciples were not of the world (v. 14). They had already received God's glory (v. 22) and God's Spirit in regeneration (John 20:22). At the Passover Feast Jesus announced that all of His disciples were clean (John 13:10), excepting Judas Iscariot. The disciples were told that their names were written in heaven and that they ought to rejoice in this knowledge (Luke 10:17-20). The fact that our Lord prayed that Peter's faith might not fail him is proof enough that Peter was not an unbeliever (Luke 22:32). Peter had already confessed his personal belief in Jesus Christ as Son of God at Caesarea (Matthew 16:16). This is the same Peter who was later filled with the Holy Ghost and became the spokesman of Pentecost (Acts 2).

Scripture further teaches that regeneration, or the new birth, was given under the Old Covenant. In Jesus' conversation with Nicodemus on the subject of the new birth He asked, "Art thou a teacher of Israel and knowest not these things?" The implication is that regeneration was an elementary truth of the Old Covenant and that a Jewish religious teacher ought to know about it. The circumcision of the heart, the creation of a new heart and spirit, the taking away of the stony heart—all of these were allusions to regeneration as taught in the Law and by the Prophets (Deuteronomy 10:16; 30:6; Isaiah 52:11; Ezekiel 18:32; 36:26). If the new birth is necessary for entering the Kingdom, and we know that it is (John 3:5), then Abraham, Isaac, and Jacob must have been born again of the Spirit for the Scriptures teach that they will be in the kingdom of God (Luke 13:28, 29). And we know that these patriarchs lived long before the Pentecostal baptism was given. And what is true for these patriarchs would also be true for all Old Testament saints. For without the regenerative power of the Holy Spirit, none could be saved.

If there is still any doubt that there is a special baptism of the Holy Spirit, distinct from the work of the Spirit in regeneration, one need only consider the experiences of the early Christians in Acts. Four passages in the Book of Acts describe an experience through which Christian believers received a baptism in the Holy Spirit. In chapter 8 we read of believers who had been won to Jesus Christ through the preaching of Philip. They had even been baptized in water. When news reached Jerusalem of these converts, Peter and John went down to Samaria and prayed for them that they might receive the Holy Spirit. For even though these Samaritan converts had been baptized in the name of the Lord Jesus, the Scriptures tell us that the Holy Spirit had not yet fallen on any of them (vv. 15-17). When Peter and John laid their hands upon them they received the Holy Ghost. The fact that this baptism in the Spirit was subsequent to these converts' commitment to Jesus Christ is undeniable. Only a theological bias or predilection to believe otherwise could lead one to mistake the clear teaching of Scripture concerning Spirit-baptism in Acts 8.

In Acts chapter 10 we read about a Gentile man named Cornelius who lived in Caesarea. Cornelius is described as a man who feared God, gave liberally to the needy, and as a man who prayed. While Peter preached the Word of God to Cornelius and his household the Holy Spirit fell on all who heard the word. Jewish Christians who had accompanied Peter to Cornelius's house could not doubt that the Holy Spirit had been poured out on these Gentiles because they heard them speaking in tongues and extolling God (vv. 44-48). It appears that Spirit-baptism came at Caesarea at the same time as conversion for they were subsequently baptized in water. Yet, Luke emphasizes that something special happened to those who believed. The Holy Spirit fell on them just as He had on the Jewish believers at Pentecost. They knew the Caesarean believers had been filled with the Spirit because they heard them speak in tongues just as the believers had at Pentecost. Two important truths were revealed to the believers at Caesarea. They now knew that the gift of Spirit-baptism was for Gentiles as well as Jews; and that even though Spirit-baptism was distinct from conversion, believers *could* receive this gift at conversion if they were open to the truth of the Word.

In Acts chapter 19 we read about twelve Ephesian believers who had received the baptism of John the Baptist (that is, the baptism of repentance), but they had not even heard about the Holy Spirit. On hearing this, Paul laid his hands upon them and they received the Holy Spirit and spoke with tongues and prophesied. Since all would have heard about a Holy Spirit, even from the Old Testament, the reference was obviously to the special Baptism of the Holy Spirit that was poured out at Pentecost and accompanied by outward signs (vv. 1-7).

The supreme evidence that there is a special Baptism in the Holy Spirit, subsequent to regeneration, is found in Luke's account of what happened on the Day of Pentecost. One hundred and twenty followers of Jesus had gathered in Jerusalem in response to the Lord's command that they tarry there until they were endued with power from heaven. These people were Christians before Pentecost. Many of them had followed Jesus for three years. They had already received the gift of Jesus, but they had not yet received the special gift of the Spirit which Jesus had promised. Nowhere in Scripture is the promise concerning Jesus and the promise concerning the gift of the Holy Spirit confused. At Pentecost the divine order was again clearly established. The believers who had gathered in the Upper Room were all filled with the Holy Ghost and began to speak in other tongues as the Spirit gave the utterance. Peter then used the occasion to make it clear to the whole multitude that conversion must precede the gift of the Holy Ghost: "Then Peter said unto them, Repent and be baptized every one of you in the name of Jesus Christ for the remission of sins, and ye shall receive the gift of the Holy Ghost" (Acts 2:38).

D. Spirit-baptism is empowerment for witness and service.

Holy Spirit baptism is not for the purpose of uniting us to Christ soteriologically (that is, redemptively). We have already noted that Jesus' disciples were redemptively united to Him before Pentecost. The purpose of Pentecost was to unite Jesus' disciples to Him vocationally. Jesus had accomplished the will of God in the power of the Holy Spirit; believers could only be the extension of Christ in the world when they too were filled with the Spirit. The church would bear witness to Christ through the Spirit just as Christ had borne witness to the Father in the power of the Spirit (Luke 24:47-49; Acts 1:8). The inactive condition of the apostolic church, even after the resurrection and post-resurrection appearances of Christ, was not altered until the Church was empowered by the Holy Spirit for its mission. When the disciples were filled with the Holy Ghost on the Day of Pentecost, they were equipped by the Spirit to be Christ's witnesses in word and deed. This is proof enough that the Holy Spirit is the only means whereby the Church can truly be the Church of the living God.

Power has always been the striking characteristic of the Baptism in the Holy Spirit. The Holy Spirit is the power through which believers witness and prophesy (Acts 1:8). God operates in His Church through the gifts of the Spirit. Hence, Pentecostals have always stressed the operation of the gifts in the church. Whenever believers are empowered and gifted by the Holy Spirit the church is enabled to continue the ministry of Christ in the world through its witness and service.

Witnessing is more than telling. It is something we are. The power of the Spirit to morally and ethically transform us ought never to be diminished in our thinking about the Holy Spirit. He is the Spirit of holiness (Romans 1:4). Witnessing and serving in the power of the Holy Spirit refers to what we are as well as what we do and say. Consequently, there must be an adequate and balanced emphasis upon the Spirit's fruit and sanctifying power in the life of the believer. For the believer's walk can never be separated from the believer's witness. Pentecost and Calvary can never be detached from one another. What each represents is an integral part of the one purpose of God for the believer and the Church.[27]

SPEAKING IN TONGUES

The doctrine that most markedly separates Pentecostals from Protestants in mainline Reformation denominations is the distinction Pentecostals make between the work of the Holy Spirit in regeneration and the Spirit's work in Spirit-baptism. The doctrine that separates Pentecostals from Wesleyan and Holiness bodies, on the other hand, is the Pentecostal teaching that speaking in other tongues as the Spirit gives the utterance is the initial physical evidence of being baptized in the Holy Ghost. When traditional Pentecostal groups raised speaking in tongues as the initial evidence of Spirit-baptism to doctrinal status, holiness denominations began to disassociate themselves from the Pentecostal movement. Tongues-speaking became the distinctive and demarcating practice of Pentecostals. This teaching and practice, more than anything else, separated Pentecostals from their holiness brethren.[28]

There is, of course, much more to Pentecostalism than speaking in tongues. But since it is such a striking feature of Pentecostal teaching and practice, and certainly one that is often misunderstood, it is important that one clearly understand what Pentecostals teach, as well as what they do not teach, about the subject.

Pentecostals believe that authentic experiences with God result in certainties, not doubts. The apostolic church could speak with boldness the things which they had seen and heard and experienced because they were convinced themselves that these things were true. An experience with God that offers assurance and certainty is an ongoing necessity for all who would give witness to the world with confidence and conviction.

God does indeed provide an inward witness of certainty through the Holy Spirit. But it is also important to know that God has provided outward empirical signs of His grace. Under the Old covenant, circumcision was the outward sign that one was a member of the covenant and shared in the promises of God to the nation. In the New Testament, water baptism became the outward sign of the New Covenant relation. God has seemingly willed to provide outward empirical signs and testimonies of the inner workings of divine grace in our lives. It should not seem strange then that God would attach the outward empirical sign of tongues to the gift of Spirit-baptism, particularly when the sign so beautifully and appropriately bespeaks its own significance for the witnessing Christian.

When the Holy Spirit was poured out at the turn of the century many Pentecostals were not sure themselves about the meaning of tongues. They had experienced it, but there were questions regarding its scriptural meaning. As they studied the Scriptures the conviction grew stronger that tongues invariably accompany baptism in the Holy Spirit. Scriptures such as Acts 2:4; 10:44-46; 19:1-7; and, to their minds, 8:14-24 provided sufficient evidence to Pentecostals that Baptism in the Holy Spirit was always signified by the "initial, physical evidence" of tongues in the New Testament.[29] This conviction was soon raised to doctrinal status and became universal among traditional Pentecostals, separating them in this point of doctrine from the main body of the holiness movement which had otherwise provided the infrastructure upon which Pentecostal theology had been built.

Many were puzzled, however, about First Corinthians 12 which clearly teaches that all do not speak with tongues.[30] How could that be reconciled with the doctrinal position that all who are baptized in the Spirit speak with tongues? Some early Pentecostals were convinced that the gift of tongues spoken of in First Corinthians 12 referred to a supernatural ability to speak in an actual (but unlearned) foreign language, and that its purpose was to preach the gospel in foreign lands. This fascination with xenoglossy, the ability to speak an unlearned foreign language, actually led several missionaries to leave for foreign lands not knowing the native language but convinced that the Holy Spirit would allow them to speak in it once they arrived. Experience and Scripture soon convinced Pentecostals that this was not the meaning of tongues spoken of in First Corinthians 12.[31] The reconciliation between the teaching of Acts and Corinthians on the subject of tongues came when Pentecostals concluded that there must be two kinds of tongues, one a sign, the other a gift. They are not different with regard to sound, but they are different with regard to function. The distinction is aptly drawn by French Arrington, a Pentecostal Bible scholar:

> A distinction may be made between . . . "devotional tongues" and the gift of tongues. The devotional tongues, which is proper for all Spirit-baptized believers, edifies only the speaker and is intended

more for private than public worship. The gift of tongues is given for public use and demands interpretation so that the local church may be edified.[32]

Another purpose for the gift of tongues, other than the edification of the church, is that they serve as a sign to unbelievers. The experience of tongues that one receives at Spirit-baptism serves as a sign to the believer that the Holy Spirit indwells that person in a special way for the purpose of being Christ's witness to the world. The gift of tongues, when interpreted, is a sign to unbelievers—just as the strange tongues of foreigners were a sign of God's judgment to the disobedient nation of Israel (1 Corinthians 14:21, 22).

Tongues are a gift of God and ought not to be forbidden nor despised (1 Corinthians 14:39). But one ought to be aware that this gift, like any other, can be easily abused. In the Corinthian Church tongues were being misused and were disruptive. Paul admonished the church to do all things in a fitting and orderly way, including the exercising of spiritual gifts.

Pentecostals are aware that their belief that speaking in tongues is the initial, physical evidence of Spirit-baptism is also highly susceptible to misunderstanding and abuse. It is important to know precisely what Pentecostals teach about this experience. They do not teach that believers should seek a "tongues experience." Believers should seek for the fullness of God's power which comes through Spirit-baptism. When that has happened the Spirit will bear evidence through unknown utterances or tongues. One ought not to confuse the sign of the reality for the reality itself. Pentecostals do not teach that speaking in tongues is the only evidence of Spirit-baptism nor that it is necessarily the most important evidence of being baptized in the Holy Spirit. They teach only that it is the initial evidence of Spirit-baptism in accordance with the biblical pattern of Acts 2:4; 10:44-46; 19:1-7. The surest sign that one is living in the power of the Holy Spirit is the lordship of Jesus Christ in the life of the Christian believer (John 16:13-15; 1 Corinthians 12:1-3). A life lived in accordance with the law of love is the Christian's highest goal (1 Corinthians 13:1-3; 14:1).

THE STRANGE WORLD OF THE SPIRIT

Disorder and confusion do not naturally follow from the work of the Holy Spirit. To the contrary, divine order and unity proceed from the presence and work of the Holy Spirit in the church. Where there is confusion and schism it is the result of carnality, not the Spirit of God. Divine order in the church, however, does not always mean what some think. The operation of the Holy Spirit in the church is always a matter of God's free grace. The Spirit's work cannot be humanly prescribed nor ordered to fit preexisting conditions or satisfy personal tastes and values. He works as He wills or else the Spirit is grieved and hindered.

Unfortunately, many Christians are not willing to have their ideas exploded or their predictable patterns of worship and lifestyle radically changed. At least not to the degree that sometimes occur when the Holy Spirit is welcomed without reservation into one's life and into the life of the church. How many in Christendom today would feel comfortable about communication with God in the language of the Spirit? How many would allow the Holy Spirit to inspire their faith to the degree that they could lay hands on the incurably ill and declare their healing? How many lives today are marked by the love, joy, and peace that follow from the Spirit's living presence? The strange world of the Spirit is much too radical for many in Christendom. Many speak of their desire for the special presence and power of the Holy Spirit in the church today. But what they really want is a Holy Spirit that has been safely brought under the control of preexisting patterns and expectations. Those who truly desire the movement of the Holy Spirit in the church today, as He moved in the apostolic church, must be open and prepared for the free movement of the Spirit.

This does not mean that the Holy Spirit will deny, contradict, or supercede the truths of Scripture. We

know that He will never do that because the Spirit of
God and the Word of God cannot be separated. They are
one in purpose. If we want to know how God wills to
move by His Spirit today and tomorrow we need only to
look into the Scriptures and discover how God willed to
move and what God willed to accomplish in the past.
There is a continuity to the eternal purpose of God. The
free action of God's grace is always in accordance with
that eternal purpose. The purpose of the Holy Spirit in
the church today is not to give us new truth but to
make the truth we have in the Word alive and operational.
Truths neatly rationalized and categorized are not enough.
Truth needs to be potent. Truth has a way of losing its
potency when it is not set aflame by the Holy Spirit.
Truth set aflame by the Holy Spirit has always been
more effective than truth preserved on ice. The Holy
Spirit does not bring us a new truth, but He does
enable us to see the old truths in a new way. For as J.
Rodman Williams reminds us, life in the Spirit means
more than a "spiritual pickup," a mere "move ahead," or
increased commitment or dedication. Baptism in the
Holy Spirit is more radical, more life changing than
that. It is not a matter of releasing power already
resident in us. Or, giving us "more" than we already
have in Christ. It is the Spirit of Christ "poured out" in
a new way. As Williams expresses it:

> To be 'filled' with the Spirit is not so much to have
> something 'more' as it is to be in the new, wonderful,
> and at times fearful situation of having the Spirit
> of God break into the whole round of existence and
> pervade it all. As a result of this —yes, explosion—
> what may be violent at the beginning can become
> the steady and driving power of a mighty dynamo—
> the Spirit of the living God.[33]

Spirit-baptism is for all who are redemptively united
to Christ. Being "filled" with the Spirit is the believer's
equipment for taking up Christ's vocation in power.
This is not an experience that happens to an institution.
It will affect institutions and institutions will become
more effective when their members are Spirit filled. But
it is an experience that is profoundly personal. To those

who seek Him, it is the Father's good pleasure to give them the Holy Spirit (Luke 11:13). When the old wine is released in new wineskins the celebration will begin to flow forth in joy and laughter.

FOOTNOTES

[1]The Assemblies of God, organized in 1914 as an amalgamation of various Pentecostal groups, was the major exception. Many in the Assemblies disliked the Wesleyan focus upon the second blessing, preferring a position more characteristic of the Reformed tradition. This "finished work" position, as it came to be called, collapsed conversion and sanctification into a single experience, followed by a second experience of baptism in the Holy Spirit, evidenced by tongues.

[2]Winthrop Hudson, *Religion in America,* 2nd ed. (New York: Charles Scribner's Sons, 1973), pp. 428-431.

[3]Ibid.

[4]John Wesley, *A Plain Account of Christian Perfection* (London: Epworth Press, 1952), p. 58.

[5]William J. O'Shea, *Sacraments of Initiation* (Englewood Cliffs: Prentice-Hall, 1965), p. 63.

[6]Ibid. p. 62

[7]Ibid. For similar views on confirmation see Karl Rahner's *A New Baptism in the Spirit: Confirmation Today* (Danville, N. J.: Dimension Books, 1975), pp. 19-20; *Foundations of Christian Faith,* pp. 416-17. Also see the chapter entitled, "The Universal Call to Holiness in the Church," in *The Sixteen Documents of Vatican II.*

[8]*John Calvin, Commentary on the Book of Acts* (Grand Rapids: Eerdmans, 1949), 2:211. Calvin's views established the pattern for the Reformed tradition.

[9]James D. G. Dunn, "Spirit-Baptism and Pentecostalism," *Scottish Journal of Theology,* XXIII (November, 1970), p. 397.

[10]Laurence W. Wood, "Thoughts Upon the Wesleyan Doctrine of Entire Sanctification with Special Reference to the Roman Catholic Doctrine of Confirmation," *Wesleyan Journal of Theology,* XV (Spring, 1980), pp. 91-92.

[11]Dunn, p. 398. The most important exponents of the "Higher Life" message were W. E. Boardman, whose book *The Higher Christian Life* (1859) had wide circulation in America and Britain, Robert Pearsall Smith, whose chief writing was *Holiness Through Faith* (1870), and his wife Hannah, whose book *The Christian's Secret of a Happy Life* (1888) is still published. The most prominent Holiness churches were The Christian and Missionary Alliance (formed in 1887), the Church of the Nazarene (formed in 1905), and The Salvation Army.

[12]Ibid., p. 400.

[13]Donald W. Dayton, "From 'Christian Perfection' to the 'Baptism of the Holy Ghost,' " in *Aspects of Pentecostal-Charismatic Origins,* ed. Vinson Synon (Plainfield, N. J.: Logos International, 1975), p. 47.

[14]Dunn, p. 400.

[15]R. A. Torrey gave the doctrine of Spirit-baptism special emphasis in his books, *The Baptism with the Holy Spirit* (1897) and *The Person and Work of the Holy Spirit* (1910). But Torrey moved away from the "purity" theme of the holiness tradition and emphasized that the baptism of the Holy Spirit was for the purpose of empowering for service. Torrey's emphasis was more congenial to the Calvinistic wing of revivalism.

[16]Donald W. Dayton, "The Doctrine of the Baptism of the Holy Spirit: Its Emergence and Significance," *Wesleyan Journal of Theology,* XIII (Spring, 1978), p. 122.

[17]Ibid.

[18]It should be pointed out that not all traditional Pentecostals insisted upon tongues as the evidence of Spirit-baptism. T. B. Barratt, the father of European Pentecostalism, maintained that many have had mighty baptisms without this sign (tongues). For a discussion of Barratt and his views, see N. Bloch-Hoell's published dissertation entitled *The Pentecostal Movement.*

[19]Minor differences among Pentecostals are too numerous to mention. The major deviance occurred in 1914 when a nontrinitarian element emerged under the name of the "Oneness" or "Jesus Only" group. The United Pentecostal Church, with its black affiliate, the Pentecostal Assemblies of the World, is the largest single Oneness body.

[20]*TWNT,*VI, p. 394.

[21]Lesslie Newbigin, *The Household of God: Lectures on the Nature of the Church* (New York: Friendship Press, 1954), p. 95.

[22]*Christian Belief* (1950), p. 56.

[23]Scholars in recent times have lauded Pentecostals for their rediscovery of the Spirit in terms of experience rather than ritual acts (baptism, confirmation) or a profession of faith. James Dunn, in particular, has called attention to the experiential aspect of the Spirit in the New testament.

[24]See G. A. Turner's "Evaluation of John R. W. Stott's and Frederick D. Bruner's Interpretations of the Baptism and Fullness of the Holy Spirit," *Wesleyan Theological Journal,* VIII (1973) pp. 45-51. The most scholarly refutation of Bruner's objectivist and sacramental interpretation of Spirit-baptism is James Dunn's work, particularly his *Baptism in the Holy Spirit.* Where Dunn differs from Pentecostals is in his view that the converting—initiating work of the Spirit ought not to be split into two distinct stages (regeneration and Spirit-baptism). The most scholarly refutation of Dunn to date, from a traditional

Pentecostal perspective, is probably Harold Hunter's recently published work *Spirit-Baptism: A Pentecostal Alternative*, University Press, 1983.

[25]J. Rodman Williams, *The Era of the Spirit* (Plainfield, New Jersey: Logos International, 1971), p. 62.

[26]Karl Barth, *Evangelical Theology*, trans. Glover Foley (New York: Doubleday and Co., 1964), p. 52. It is instructive to note that the Greek *lambanein* (to accept) is invariably used whenever the Holy Spirit is the object received. The term infers that the Holy Spirit is accepted by direct choice of will. In the following texts the forcible, active, transitive verb *lambanein* (to accept, take, choose, seize) is used without exception: John 7:38, 39; 14:17, 20, 22; Acts 2:38; 8:15, 17; 10:47; 19:2; Romans 8:15; 1 Corinthians 2:12; Galatians 3:2, 14; 1 John 2:24; Revelation 22:17. In ten of these texts *lambanein* is in the aorist. In texts where the passive idea of "receive" is expressed (Acts 3:21; 2 Corinthians 5:10) *dechomai*, *Konizo*, or some other verb admitting the passive idea is used. For an excellent exposition on the use of *lambanein* see Thomas Payne's *The Pentecostal Baptism: Is it Regeneration?* (London), pp. 13-25.

[27]In their emphasis upon Spirit-baptism as empowerment for witness and service, Pentecostals ought not allow the ethical and moral purpose of the Spirit to be diminished. One does not fully understand the purpose of the Spirit from Acts alone. The missionary emphasis of Acts must be balanced with the ethical and moral emphasis of the Pauline Epistles.

[28]Carl Brumback, *Suddenly from Heaven: A History of the Assemblies of God* (Springfield Mo.: Gospel Publishing House, 1961), p. 23.

[29]The Scriptures do not specifically say that the Samaritan believers spoke in tongues when they received the Holy Spirit. However, it is instructive to note that something happened which allowed them to know that they had indeed received the Holy Ghost. Whatever it was, Simon saw it and desired to buy it with money. It was obviously an outward empirical sign, and Pentecostals are convinced it was the sign of tongues.

[30]In 1 Corinthians 12:30 Paul asks, "Do all speak with tongues?" He does not specifically say that they do not, but his use of the negative (me) anticipates a negative answer.

[31]The initial fascination with xenoglossy among Pentecostals soon disappeared. Pentecostals generally agreed that while the gift of tongues can be miraculously manifested as an actual language, this is not the normal function of tongues. The normal function of the gift of tongues is that which Paul teaches in 1 Corinthians; namely, the edification of the church through interpretation and as a sign to unbelievers.

[32]French Arrington, *Divine Order in the Church* (Cleveland, Tenn.: Pathway Press, 1978), p. 132.

[33]Williams, p. 55.

Chapter 5

The Holy Spirit and Power

The Purpose of Power

Power is a word that is virtually synonymous with Spirit. The Holy Spirit is God's power in action. Whenever the Holy Spirit is mentioned in Scripture, there is usually some corresponding reference or allusion to God's power. The Holy Spirit is God's creative and life-giving power. He is the power that inspires prophecy, the power behind miracles and extraordinary phenomenon, the power that underlies God's purpose. The Holy Spirit is also moral power, the power of holiness and righteousness at work in the believer effecting God's salvific purpose and raising up a moral standard.

In the Old Testament the Spirit often seized a person or was given to a person for a particular situation or task. The Spirit gave that person a special character or imparted a supernatural quality to their nature, enduing them with the physical or moral ability necessary for the accomplishment of God's purpose. When the Holy Spirit came at Pentecost, His presence and power in the believer was more permanent. He made Christ present and real in the experience of believers and equipped them with power for witness and service.

The power of the Holy Spirit has always been related to God's purpose. The Spirit's power was never given nor demonstrated merely to amuse or impress the creature but to transform human life and shape history in accordance with the divine will. Jesus' use of power in the New Testament is for us the ultimate example of its purposeful and responsible use. Jesus never used His power in a capricious way. The Spirit's power always operated purposefully in the life and ministry of Jesus. Jesus' mighty deeds were visible signs that the New Age was present. In the power of the Holy Spirit, Jesus healed the sick, cast out demons, and triumphed over the rule of Satan. Jesus did not exercise His power in order to prove His deity or to bring about His kingdom. On the contrary, the power of the Spirit in Jesus was the sign that God's kingdom was already present, that God's purpose was being fulfilled. God confirmed the arrival of the New Age and the announcement of the gospel through His Son with "signs" and "wonders." The power of the Holy Spirit was the sign that the messianic age had arrived.

The resurrection of Jesus through the power of the Spirit was the sign of all signs, the wonder of all wonders. Those who refused to acknowledge this sign could not be won by any other. Divine power was a witness to the power of the gospel. Power was not something tied to the gospel for extra effect. It was an essential part of the gospel itself—a message to all that God's purpose was being effected through God's power. Those who doubt the life-giving power of the gospel, or weaken its message by adopting reductionist theories which strip it of its miraculous and supernatural character, miss an essential element in the gospel message.

EMPOWERMENT FOR MISSION

The power through which Jesus announced the "good news" of the kingdom of God was the power of the Holy Spirit. The importance of the Spirit's power in relation to believers can be seen in its importance for those whom God calls and commissions into His service. Power is necessary for the transmission of the gospel message. God never calls men and women to be or to do that for which He does not empower them. When Christ sent His disciples forth, He gave them power and authority over all demonic power.[1] Luke says that, "He called His twelve disciples together and gave them power and authority over all demons, and to cure diseases. He sent them to preach the kingdom of God and to heal" (Luke 9:1, 2, *NKJ*; see also 10:19). The power in which Jesus initiated the Kingdom was given the Twelve and was later promised to all those who would continue Jesus' ministry in the world after the ascension:

> You are witnesses of these things. And behold, I send the promise of my Father upon you; but stay in the city, *until you are clothed with power* from on high (Luke 24:48, 49; *RSV*).

> *You shall receive power* when the Holy Spirit has come upon you; and you shall be witnesses to me in Jerusalem, and in all Judea and Samaria, and to the end of the earth (Acts 1:8, *NKJ*).

Being endowed or clothed with power for witness is never presented in the New Testament as an optional experience for Christian believers.[2] The believer cannot be the extension of Christ in the world, as Christ intended, until he has been properly attired with the Spirit. The church cannot effectively exist as a worshiping or a witnessing community apart from the Spirit's enduement of power. The church existed before Pentecost, but it lacked motivation and power. It was an inactive church. It was not properly equipped. What the church needed to fulfill the Great Commission was the power of the Holy Spirit. When the New Testament church received its enduement of power at Pentecost it immediately became a witnessing and serving church. The power of the Holy Spirit has always been that which is necessary to the church's mission in the world.

POWER FOR PROCLAMATION

The promised enduement of power for witness came on the Day of Pentecost. Particularly noticeable in the pattern that unfolds in Acts is the relationship between power and witness (proclamation). The first event recorded after Pentecost was the healing of the lame man at the gate of the Temple. The account of this healing, however, does not stand alone. It leads to the question on the part of the rulers, "By what Power or by what name have you done this?" Peter then gives witness to Christ, "By the name of Jesus Christ of Nazareth, whom you crucified, whom God raised from the dead" (Acts 4:7-10, *NKJ*).

Miracles are commonplace in Acts. But they are more than displays of power. They provide opportunities and forums for witness. The power that manifests itself in miraculous deeds is also present within the disciples. It gives them courage and a desire to proclaim Jesus Christ. Luke tells us that, *"With great power* the apostles *gave their testimony* to the resurrection of the Lord Jesus, and great grace was upon them all" (Acts 4:33, *RSV*).

The ministry of Paul fits the same pattern. His ministry was one of proclamation with power. To the Corinthians, Paul preached, "In demonstration of the Spirit and power" (1 Corinthians 2:4, *RSV*). He reminded the Thessalonians that the "gospel came . . . not only in word, but also in power and in the Holy Spirit and with full conviction" (1 Thessalonians 1:5, *RSV*). To the Romans, Paul wrote that he would "not venture to speak of anything except what Christ has wrought through me . . . by word and deed, by the power of signs and wonders, by the power of the Holy Spirit" (Romans 15:18, 19)

Paul knew from experience the presence of the exalted Lord, the power of the New Age through the Spirit. But Paul's great discovery was that God's power is made manifest through the weakness of the Cross. Paul's desire was to establish believers in God's saving power through the preaching of the Cross. But he faced a battle on two fronts. One battle was with the Jews who trusted in the righteousness of the Law instead of the righteousness of Christ. The other battle was with the Greeks who trusted in false knowledge and wisdom. The Cross was an offense to both; it could not be reconciled with either Jewish legalism or Greek wisdom. Against both, Paul preached the wisdom and saving power of the Cross.

Power cannot be separated from the gospel—for the same Christ who gave Himself to be crucified in weakness was raised from the dead by the power of the Spirit. Whenever the word of the Cross is preached, God confirms the power of the Cross by giving new life to those who believe. The weakness of God is stronger than the might of men. Through weakness, Paul discovered that God can manifest strength. God's power is manifest through the weakness of the Cross, and it is also manifest through the weakness of the messenger. For in the confessed weakness of our own person, we find the strength of the person of the Holy Spirit who bears witness to Jesus.

POWER AND SUFFERING

The irony of power is that it is essential to the gospel's success, and yet it is the one thing that most easily corrupts. A desire for power without the cross always brings corruption and carnality. Paul knew the danger in knowing Christ "in the power of His resurrection" without a willingness to identify with Him "in His suffering." One cannot claim the authority of Jesus unless he is willing to identify with the Cross and accept its judgment on all forms of human power and wisdom. No person can be trusted with power, not even spiritual power, who cannot emulate Jesus' use of power on the Cross.

Power was a particular concern for the New Testament church, the "New Israel," because it had been born and commissioned in power. The resurrection of Jesus and the subsequent sending of the Spirit at Pentecost made the church aware of the newly released power in which they were living and carrying out their vocation as the people of God. The liberating power of the Spirit over sin and death and the alien powers of this world gave the early church a unique experience of abounding power. But the experience of power also contained a threat. The Spirit-filled community had to be most careful at the point of its spiritual success. The Corinthian believers were a case in point. They were richly gifted by the Spirit, but their abuse of power and of spiritual gifts was threatening the life of this congregation. Paul's message to the Corinthians was that the power of the Holy Spirit is the Spirit of the crucified Jesus (1 Corinthians 1:17-31). A Christian community must always live at the foot of the Cross. The body of Christ is, as the Lord's Supper reminds us, a broken body.[3]

The irony of power was evident in Paul's personal calling and ministry. Paul was an apostle, a chosen vessel of God, called to carry the name of Christ before Gentiles and kings. For such a task, Paul needed the power of the Holy Spirit. He preached the gospel in power, and God confirmed the message with signs and wonders. But even before Ananias laid his hands upon Paul that he might regain his sight and receive the Holy Spirit, the Lord of the Church instructed Ananias that Paul would suffer for Christ's name (Acts 9:16). The purpose for God's power in Paul would be to bring others to the realization of God's righteousness. Paul was to understand from the beginning that persecution and suffering are coterminous with righteousness in a world that is ruled by the power of sin. Paul later instructed Timothy that "All who will live godly in Christ Jesus shall suffer persecution" (2 Timothy 3:12). Throughout his ministry, Paul suffered persecution and affliction. But he gloried in the power of the Cross. The Cross was, for Paul, the power to triumph over cheap grace, the power to rejoice in prison, to suffer deprivation, to count everything as loss for the surpassing worth of knowing Jesus as Lord.

The other apostles also experienced the irony of suffering power. As they preached the gospel, signs and wonders followed. The spoken word was confirmed by the power of the New Age. Miraculous healings occurred (Acts 3); evil spirits were exorcized (Acts 16:16-18); a young boy was restored to life (Acts 29:9-12). But the triumph of the gospel did not exempt them from persecution and suffering. Peter, in the first half of Acts, and Paul, in the latter, were in prison as often as they were in public. Power in Acts is portrayed throughout as power in the midst of suffering.[4]

After periods of persecution the church found it necessary to gather for fresh infillings of power and boldness from the Holy Spirit (Acts 4:31, 33; 5:32). But after gathering together and receiving fresh power and boldness, the church always scattered again, preaching the gospel and fulfilling its mission. The church never stayed huddled together too long for the sake of security and serenity. Acts ends on a note that is characteristic of the whole tenor of the book. Paul is in Rome preaching an "unhindered" gospel (28:31); yet he is "in chains" (28:20; 12:6, 7; 21:33).

THE EXAMPLE OF JESUS

The apostolic church seemingly had a more profound appreciation for the powers of the New Age than Christians of any other time. But just as important, they seemed to understand the relationship between power and suffering. For whatever reasons this was true, one reason seems clear. The early church was close to the time of Jesus; the memory of His example was still fresh. In times of persecution and suffering, the church remembered the example of Jesus who suffered for righteousness' sake. The sacrament of the Supper which Jesus instituted was a continual reminder that Christ's body was a broken body, a suffering body. During the Neronian persecution the Apostle Peter reminded suffering Christians that, "To this you have been called [to suffer for righteousness sake], because Christ also suffered for you, leaving you an example, that you should follow in his steps" (1 Peter 2:21; 2:11-25).

Jesus' obedience in fulfilling His mission was an obedience of suffering (Hebrews 5:8; Philippians 2:9-11; Revelation 5:12). Every baptism into Christ is a baptism into His death. This is what Christian baptism symbolizes. In baptism we are "planted together in the likeness of his death" (Romans 6:5; Philippians 3:10). Only through crucifixion with Christ can the believer find new life and a new identity with Him (Galatians 5:24; Romans 6:6; Colossians 3:3; Ephesians 4:22). The Cross is the supreme test of discipleship (Mark 8:34, 35). A willingness to deny self and suffer for righteousness is tantamount to being Jesus' disciple.

The straight way which Jesus invites His followers to travel is no broadway of "easy-believism." Early Christians were called "followers of the way" because Christianity was a way—a way which Jesus had traveled before them. John the Baptist came preparing the way with his message of the coming kingdom and its demand for repentance. Repentance (metanoia) meant radical change, a reversal of one's thinking, and a willingness to follow a new way. It was inconceivable that one would choose to follow the way of Jesus without a radical change of mind, affections, and will.

When Jesus appeared, He did not preach soothing sermons. He announced (that is, proclaimed) the kingdom of God that was present and accessible to faith through the Spirit. Jesus urged men to repent and believe the gospel. Those who repented and received the good news of the Kingdom were expected to announce it to others. All are called to bear witness to the reality of the New Age. The New Testament word for "witnessing" is martyria from which we get our English word martyr. Witnessing in a New Testament context means pointing to a reality that is costly in every respect. God's gift-love was costly in terms of what it cost God. It was not "cheap" grace. It was costly for Christ who made the supreme sacrifice, and it was costly for His followers who sealed their testimony with their own blood. Tradition tells us that only one of the Twelve died a natural death. The others were martyred for their faith. The cost was high, but the blood of the martyrs became the seed of the Church.

It is against the backdrop of God's gracious offer of forgiveness and entrance into His kingdom through the Holy Spirit that the "sin against the Holy Spirit" can be understood. The sin against the Holy Spirit of which Jesus spoke and the lie to the Holy Spirit which resulted in the death of Ananias and Sapphira were the radical consequences of rejecting God's provision of grace. To attribute God's provision of grace to evil and knowingly attempt to thwart the power and reality of the New Age is not an alternative to be exercised without serious consequence. To whom much is given, much is required.

Christianity is lavish in what it promises, but it is also radical in what it demands. It promises a pearl of great price but only at the cost of selling all other pearls in the collection. Finding Christ is like finding treasure in an open field for which one is willing to sell all that he has and buy the field (Matthew 13:44-46). What one is freely promised is saved from cheapness by the radical demand that one follow in the way that Jesus has already traveled.

Christianity is not a masochistic religion that values "suffering for suffering sake." There is no pleasure or sense of rightness to be derived merely from suffering. It has no inherent virtue. The Christian does not suffer because he feels it is his duty to suffer. He suffers because of his solidarity with a fallen human race, because he lives in an unjust world, controlled by evil alien powers, where there is for the "seeker after righteousness" an inevitable relationship between suffering and righteousness. Whoever takes righteousness for his goal in this life ought to be prepared to suffer for it. For all the forces of this world oppose it. Dietrich Bonhoeffer, the German theologian who was martyred by the Third Reich for his faith, warned that, "When Christ calls a man, he bids him come and die." Karl Barth said that the first three petitions of the prayer which Jesus taught His disciples to pray, "Thy name," "Thy kingdom," and "Thy will," are equivalent to the saying: "Teach us to reflect that we must die."

There is a philosophy among some that Christians need never suffer or be deprived of any material good. They preach a gospel of health, wealth, and prosperity. Christians can have as much as they have faith to name and claim. The doctrine is attractive because it seems to promise what we want. But it is nothing more than a current fad. It is unbiblical and totally out of keeping with traditional Christianity. A "you get what you speak" philosophy elevates a faith-in-faith mindset above the sovereignty of God's will and purpose. Biblical realism knows nothing of a positive state of mind which produces a fact. It is not the purpose of faith to manipulate God and His will. Faith is an obedient response to the will of God who works all things together according to His eternal purpose. A theology that makes no distinction between what we wish was the case and what we are forced, by the facts, to believe is the case is shallow and subjectivist. It is harmful to the believer and belies factual realism. Authentic Christian experience must be grounded in God's truth, not self-hypnosis. One of the truths upon which authentic Christian experience rests is the truth of the Cross. It is not just Jesus' cross that concerns us but our own. Cross bearing will always be an inevitable fact for the Christian because he lives at cross purposes with this world.

The Christian is not totally altruistic when he commits to a way that involves suffering. Suffering and dying to self are not ends in themselves. They are the means to the highest possible form of human happiness. The Christian does not suffer out of a martyr's complex, or for duty sake, but for the sake of the righteousness he seeks—the righteousness of Christ. A Christian is not denying his true self when he willingly suffers for that which is the highest attainable good. He is really seeking his highest self. Christians are goal-seekers; they are pilgrims who are convinced that righteousness is the highest good. One will not be preoccupied with the light afflictions of this present age if he has a clear vision of the end toward which he is moving. Bonhoeffer wrote from prison, "In the light of our supreme purpose our personal privations and disappointments seem trivial." Suffering and death are constant reminders, both for ourselves and those we love, that the final goal we seek is still ahead of us. To see ourselves aright, we must always see our good in light of our end. For the sake of the eternal life we partly already know, we glimpse the glory of that which is ahead. And for the sake of it, we die daily that we may someday inherit it in its fullness.

POWER TO SERVE

The irony of "power that can suffer" was foolish to Greek wisdom and discontinuous with Jewish expectations of a messiah who would establish a kingdom through power. Jesus' life and ministry was itself an example of two things necessary for the Church: power and service.

Jesus was no romantic. He knew the realities of power and did not bypass its use in His own ministry. The Spirit was the divine power in which Jesus confronted the forces of darkness which stood in opposition to the kingdom of God. One of the major motifs in the Gospel of Mark is the way Jesus faced conflict with demons and Pharisees and triumphed over them in the power of the Spirit (Mark 1:16—8:21). Yet, Jesus did not have the spirit of triumphal-"ism." His ultimate triumph did not come through miracles. It came through the most unlikely form—the Cross. Signs of power were evidence that the Age to Come was already present through the Spirit. But signs and wonders were not meant to be the basis for faith. Miracles and power alone could not turn Jesus' followers into genuine disciples; Jesus wanted true disciples who would take up their cross and follow Him.

Power was necessary for the accomplishment of Jesus' vocation. He did not shun its use. All that Jesus accomplished was in the power of the Holy Spirit. The problem that Jesus faced, however, was the problem inherent in the use of any form of spiritual power. Namely, "how shall the power be used?" We are all aware that political power can corrupt politicians. Economic power can be used to exploit and oppress. Military power can be used to dominate and enslave. The consequences of misusing these harder forms of power are more obvious to us than the misuse of the softer forms. But the latter can be just as sinister and devious as the former. Those who are gifted with a good mind constantly face the temptation to misuse its power for selfish fame and fortune. The person with extraordinary talent always struggles with the temptation to misuse it. Those with strong and dynamic personalities must always guard against the tendency to win by force of personality that which ought to be won by force of character and good will. What Christians do not often realize is that spiritual power can also be abused. All forms of power which are not controlled by the love and righteousness of God can and will corrupt.[5] Even Jesus had to face the problems that are associated with power.

This issue had to be settled at the beginning of Jesus' ministry. Almost immediately after the Spirit settled upon Jesus at His baptism, the Spirit led Jesus into the wilderness to face the realities and temptations of power. His strategy for ministry was to be settled in the wilderness at the outset of His ministry.[6] There He met and overcame the temptations associated with the misuse of power. He was tempted to use His power to meet material needs that would have obscured the Father's purpose for Jesus' life. Jesus knew that His life depended upon God's purpose, not upon bread. Regardless of outward circumstances, God had spoken His word concerning Jesus and Jesus found His security in God's promise. He would live because God willed it. He refused to use His power and authority for personal reasons. Jesus trusted the authority of God's Word for His security even more than the "staff of life" (that is, bread) itself.

The desire for financial and material security is a driving force within many today. The threat of an insecure future can lead a wavering and fearful Christian into an unnatural state of anxiety and desperation. There is a normal concern for material security that is needful and wise, but there is also an inordinate concern that leads some to compromise God's purpose for the promise of bread. The Christian lives by the promise and purpose of God for his life. He does not live by the vain and fleeting securities offered by Satan.

The second temptation took the form of an appeal to instant success. Satan tried to lure Jesus into a public demonstration of His power by leaping from the pinnacle of the Temple, knowing that the angels would bear Him up. This was the temptation to misuse His privilege. Would Jesus use His power in a magic-like display in order to get a quick following, or would He choose instead the slow, patient, working out of God's purpose in His life through daily contact with people? He left us the proper example by choosing the latter. Jesus rejected the misuse of personality power and cheap techniques as a way to advance God's cause with instant success.

The third temptation was to bow the knee to Satan. No one need know what happens in the wilderness. Jesus was promised worldly power and glory in return for His loyalty and worship to Satan. This temptation most seriously threatened the vocation of Jesus for whomever a person serves, to him that person belongs. This was the principle at work in this temptation. It was the same kind of existential choice that confronts us all every day. Had Jesus yielded, it would have obscured His relationship to God and served to deny the power He possessed as the divine Son of God. We always deny our true identity as children of God when we serve Satan. Satan would have liked nothing better than a trade-off—to set Jesus up as a leader of humanity in return for Jesus' denial of His relation to the Father. But Jesus rebuked the devil and refused to compromise His identity. One of the great temptations of our day is to trade off our true identity for worldly success.

Jesus modeled the same mature, responsible use of power in His training of the Twelve. As divine Son of God, Jesus was Lord. Yet He did not use His power of position to dominate. We seek to dominate each other when we are uncertain of our own identity and calling. But Jesus knew His status so perfectly that He was not threatened by the recognition of others. Because He knew who He was, Jesus was free to serve others—to confer more recognition on others than He required for Himself. This is why He could joyfully wash His disciples' feet (John Chapter 13). In a world such as ours where individuals compete for status, the status of a master depends upon his having servants and slaves, but Jesus is a different kind of Lord and Master. His Lordship is assured by His person, not by the recognition given Him by others. Lordship was not something conferred upon Jesus by followers. Jesus was Lord by nature. Knowing who He was, Jesus was freed from the struggles for prestige and status. Only those who have been freed from the struggle for prestige and superiority over others are truly freed for service. This is why it is so important for us to know that in Jesus Christ we have been accepted by God. He has made us His sons and daughters. This is the status we enjoy which sets us free for a life of service.

Jesus never commands in order to dominate or bind. His commands, as Lord, are for the purpose of setting us free. Christ commands us in order to free us. He confers sonship on us and allows us to experience the reality of sonship (Romans 8:16) in order that we may know who we are (our status) and enter into a life of service. Those who truly know who they are in Jesus Christ are set free from striving and competing with others for superiority and recognition. They are converted to their neighbor as well as to Christ.

Christ's Lordship is never destructive nor degrading for us. He gives us value before we have any value. He accepts us by grace simply because He loves us with a self-giving love (agape) and then cares for us as His own. Our life together with Christ in the kingdom does not demand a uniformity of personalities or needs. He cares for us as unique persons. As Lord, He assures us that we have no need to live with worry and anxiety for He cares much more for us than He does for the raven or the beautiful lilies of the field which neither toil nor spin (Luke 12:22-32).

The authenticity of Jesus' existence as Lord gave His teachings an unquestionable authority for those who knew Him. There was never any discrepancy between what Jesus taught and what Jesus was in His relations with others. The power of His divine Sonship was made manifest through His loving service. From the example of Jesus the church learns the meaning of power and authority. It learns what it means to be strong enough to serve, how to be a servant leader. When the church models what it teaches, it is not difficult to get a hearing. The church today is no more perfect than Jesus' closest disciples who were tempted to misuse the power of God to call down fire on their enemies. But the model for the incarnate life of the church has been manifested in Jesus Christ. The church can never say that it has not been shown what to do with the power of God.

THE POWER OF THE CROSS

In conclusion, we return to the Cross. For the Cross was the greatest test of Jesus' power, and it is the perpetual judgment on all who would abuse power. Power from a Christian perspective is always crucified power. Atonement cannot be abstracted from self-giving service, as Jesus exemplified in His own life and ministry. Jesus' death and resurrection were meant to make it possible for humankind to live as Jesus lived and serve as Jesus served. In Jesus Christ, God triumphs over suffering and death by taking them unto Himself, by overcoming evil with good. His love ultimately triumphs over all alien powers.

On the Cross, Jesus was abandoned unto death. Not even Job was tested that far. Yet, He refused to exercise His power in any way that was not in keeping with His vocation. He came into the world to die, and die He would. But through His own example, Jesus condemned forever the abuse of power. Jesus was no masochist. He did not enjoy the cruel preparation or the excruciating torments of the tree. He endured the Cross; He despised the shame (Hebrews 12:2). Yet, His final act was one of self-surrender. In the ultimate crises, He exemplified love for others and a responsible use of power that forever stands as an example and a judgment on all human activity. When the church models the same responsible, mature use of power that Jesus modeled, it is free to be the mature and powerful church that God intended.

The one thing most necessary for the success of the church is power. Without it, the church can do nothing. Without power the church is paralyzed and ineffective. Human history records for us man's struggle for power in its many different secular forms—political, economic, military, and so forth. But the need for spiritual and moral power is no less real in the church than the need for power in the world. For while the church's struggle does not call for the power to overcome "flesh and blood," it does call for power to overcome the principalities and powers that rule this present evil world (Ephesians 6:10-18). God has not left His church powerless. The church has been empowered by the Holy Spirit so that it can make its assault against the devil and the forces of evil (Matthew 16:18).

The church can only be successful in its calling to be the extension of Christ in the world when it is empowered by the same power as Jesus. Jesus came in power as the lion of Judah. In the power of the Holy Spirit He exorcized demons, healed the sick, and took authority over every force that stood opposed to the kingdom of God. Because he had "all power," Jesus could teach its proper use through precept and example. From His position of strength, Jesus taught us its mature and responsible use. He showed us how power was meant to be used in our vocation as Christians.

The problem connected with power is that it so easily corrupts. In very subtle ways, power can corrupt human personalities and institutions. It so easily moves men to manipulate and dominate, rather than serve. It moves men to seek to accomplish through the force of personality and position what can more rightly be accomplished through the force of character and good will. It leads men to think that they should always triumph over suffering when God wills that we should sometimes triumph through suffering.

Jesus did not deny power; He redeemed power. He showed us its purpose. He showed us what God meant His power to be used for in our lives. Power is a word that is almost synonymous with Pentecost. For that reason, it is all the more important that Spirit-filled Christians know its meaning. Our witness to Jesus Christ is strongest when we allow the Spirit's power to be exercised in us as it was in Jesus. In a "me-ism" generation, where selfism abounds, and men eagerly seek to live by easy success formulas we need to let Jesus teach us again what it means to be a person-for-others. We need to learn again what it means to possess the power to deny self, to know what it means to be a gentle giant.

FOOTNOTES

[1]Power (δύναμις) and authority (ἐξουσία) have closely related meanings in the New Testament. Power is almost always linked with the energy of the Holy Spirit and is often related to miraculous power. In Luke it is associated with the historical ministry of Jesus and the present life of the Church. Authority refers more to potential power, the power of delegated authority. The Scriptures speak of Satan's power (ἐξουσία) over the world, but this is a power that he does not possess in his own right (Luke 22:53; Acts 26:18). The authority which Jesus possesses and can impart is superior to the "power" of the enemy. See Hans Conzelmann, *The Theology of St. Luke*, trans. Geoffrey Buswell (New York: Harper and Row, 1961), pp. 180-184.

[2]Being endowed or clothed with power comes from the Greek word ἐνδύω which means to " dress with power" or "furnish with capacity." What the believer does in the power of the Holy Spirit is according to the capacity that God furnishes.

[3]This theme is brilliantly treated by Daniel Jenkins in *Christian Maturity and the Theology of Success* (Naperville, Illinois: SCM Book Club, 1976).

[4]Pentecostals and charismatics do tend sometimes to overlook this fact. An emphasis upon power can easily lead to an attitude of easy triumphalism, as Frederick Bruner warns in *A Theology of the Holy Spirit*. There is a balanced perspective, however, which I believe Bruner has missed in his attempt to emphasize Luther's theologia crucis (theology of the Cross). It is a balance that recognizes the necessity for divine power in the mission and operation of the Church while acknowledging that it is in our weakness that we are made strong (2 Corinthians 12:10).

[5]Between the two chapters dealing with spiritual gifts (1 Corinthians chapters 12 and 14), Paul found it necessary to insert the great chapter on love (1 Corinthians chapter 13). This, I think, is very instructive for us today.

[6]In his great poem, *Paradise Regained*, John Milton shows that Jesus' greatest victory came in the beginning of His ministry. He regained what Adam lost through the manner in which He faced the great temptations. His ministry was established at the outset by His response to Satan's temptations.

Chapter 6

The Holy Spirit as Teacher, Helper and Discipler

The Indwelling Teacher

God has many external witnesses but there is only one indwelling Teacher. God may use the testimony of a miracle to authenticate a divine work or He may use a completed prophecy to confirm the Word. The miracle is a divine work in the sphere of nature; the completion of prophecy is a providential work in the sphere of history. These evidences by which God confirms His Word to the believer and makes unbelievers responsible for rejecting His revelation are by nature external witnesses. But there is another way in which God manifests His truth to the believer as He does not manifest it to the world: that is through the internal witness of the Holy Spirit which provides the believer with a far greater certainty than any external witness possibly could. It is this witness that has enabled millions of Christians, even under adverse circumstances, to say with the writers of the New Testament, "I know whom I have believed," and " I know that all things work together for good to them that love God."

The importance of the indwelling Teacher is alluded to throughout the Scriptures. The psalmist prayed that God would open his eyes that he might behold wondrous things out of His Law (Psalm 119:18). Isaiah prophesied a time when God's children would be "taught of the Lord" (Isaiah 54:13), Jeremiah when they would "know the Lord" (Jeremiah 31:34). The healing of the blind man in the Gospels of Mark and Luke teaches the supernatural power of Jesus to heal the blind eyes of the soul (Mark 8:16-22; Luke 18:35-43). But it is in the fourteenth, fifteenth and sixteenth chapters of the Gospel of John that the truth of the indwelling Teacher is most fully developed.

Jesus' departure was a momentous event in the history of redemption. His revealing and saving work would be carried on by the Holy Spirit whom Jesus called "another Comforter." Christ's presence in His Church was meant to continue through the Holy Spirit whom Jesus said was the "Spirit of truth" (John 14:26; 15:26; 16:12). The Holy Spirit would be the indwelling Teacher who would bear witness to the departed Jesus and verify the truth of His Word. The Spirit is represented in John's Gospel as a Teacher, a Witness, a Comforter, and a Guide. In this departing discourse Jesus assures His disciples that the Spirit of truth will abide in them and be with them; that He shall teach them all things; that He will bear witness to Christ; that He shall guide them into the truth; that He shall take the things of Christ and declare them unto them.

THE DIVINE ILLUMINATOR

One area of agreement between Protestants and Roman Catholics has been the belief that God has willed to reveal His truth to men through the supernatural means of the Bible. There is a major disagreement, however, concerning the manner in which God wills to allow this revelation to pass into the life of the believer. The Roman Catholic church holds that the Bible was given to the church; that it was deposited with the church in man's behalf; that the church authenticates the teachings of the Bible by her testimony; that it is the responsibility of the church to interpret it for man according to her heavenly wisdom.

Only recently has the Roman Catholic church encouraged its lay members to read the Bible. For centuries Catholics saw the Bible as a book filled with riddles and mysteries that could only be understood and interpreted by the official clergy. Early in the history of the church the bishops were given the teaching authority, and what was passed on to the people was presented largely through imagery and pageantry. The word-centered ministry of the New Testament was soon replaced with icons, statues, and architecture designed for a teaching purpose. In essence the church soon made itself the teacher, the inspired and infallible interpreter of the Word of God.

One of the strongest affirmations of Protestantism, on the other hand, has been that God's supernatural revelation, as it is contained in the Bible, is addressed directly to man. The Bible does not have to be authenticated and interpreted by the church. The Bible is its own witness. Through the inward testimony of the Holy Spirit the believer is enabled to gain a full persuasion and assurance that the Bible is indeed the infallible truth of God. It was this conviction that led to the Protestant affirmation of the priesthood of all believers.

Through the Holy Spirit God illuminates and confirms in our hearts (that is, our understanding) what He has revealed outwardly and objectively in the form of Scripture. The foundation of our faith would indeed be frail and unsteady if it rested on human wisdom for man is finite and sinful. Man's creatureliness cannot cross the chasm that separates a finite man from an infinite God. The element of sinfulness in man renders him incapable of coming to God or penetrating God's truths because man's sin causes him to stand in opposition to God. The mysteries of the Word always lie beyond our rational comprehension. But what the Holy Spirit illuminates, the mind can grasp. The Scriptures are always sufficiently clear and comprehensible if we have the Holy Spirit as our Teacher. God's truth is not grasped without the use of the mind for there is always a reasoning process at work in man. But a mind that has been transformed and renewed by the Holy Spirit is raised above its own understanding. The Holy Spirit does not circumvent the rational processes but works through them and rises above them.

Without the illumination of the Holy Spirit the Word of God has no effect in our lives. But through the illumination of the Holy Spirit the sin-darkened mind of man can be made to comprehend what God has clearly set before him in Scripture. Through the inner work of the Holy Spirit God himself instructs us in the Christian faith.

THE DIVINE PERSUADER

In addition to being an illuminator, the Holy Spirit is also a persuader—sealing the truth of the Word to our hearts. The Holy Spirit restores a spiritual sense in the soul by which God is recognized in His Word. In Ephesians 1:13 Paul refers to the "sealing" of the Holy Spirit whereby that which God has offered outwardly and objectively in the Word is confirmed in our hearts. In his *Commentary on Galatians and Ephesians,* John Calvin explained the significance of sealing:

> . . . seals give validity to letters and testaments. . . . In short, a seal distinguishes what is genuine and certain from what is false and spurious. This office Paul ascribes to the Holy Spirit. Our minds never become so firmly established in the truth of God as to resist all the temptations of Satan [to doubt] until we have been confirmed in it by the Holy Spirit.[1]

Obscurity and doubt remain where the Holy Spirit has not illuminated and sealed the truth of God. All human arguments fail to persuade us of the truth of God; carnal reason can never be the basis for true faith in God. The only sufficient witness to God is the indwelling Spirit. The certainty which the Spirit produces in us is not a-rational or irrational but supra-rational. The knowledge of faith consists more of a certainty (persuasion) than a comprehension. It is not a "natural" reason, but it is the human mind as enlightened and persuaded by the divine Teacher that knows that which has been revealed by the Holy Spirit.

Faith which the Holy Spirit inspires in us is not a blind or groundless faith. No amount of external evidence will make a man a Christian, but it does not follow that faith will arise apart from all evidence. The Holy Spirit does not work in opposition to Christian evidences but in conjunction with them. Without some valid grounds for faith, it cannot arise. The witness of the Holy Spirit is not itself the ground of faith. "What this witness of the Spirit does," Benjamin Warfield says, "is 'fully to persuade us' that 'the Scriptures are the very Word of God,'—to work in us 'full persuasion and assurance of the infallible truth and divine authority' of the Word of God. It is a matter of completeness of conviction, not of grounds of conviction: and the testimony of the Spirit works, therefore, not by adding additional grounds of conviction, but by an inward work on the heart, enabling it to react upon the already 'abundant evidence' with a really 'full persuasion and assurance.' "[2]

THE UNITY OF WORD AND SPIRIT

The testimony of the Holy Spirit does not take the place of the objective revelation of the Word. It is not in this strict sense a revelation. The work of the Spirit presupposes the revelation given in the Scriptures and serves to prepare the heart to respond to and embrace the Word. The divine authority of the Bible is self-authenticating. But, as we have noted, it is self-authenticating only to those who have been empowered by the Spirit to perceive this authentication. Sugar is sweet whether we taste it or not. Yet its sweetness is authenticated only to those who are able to taste it. Blue is blue regardless of the trustworthiness of our own sight. Yet the color blue is only authenticated for those who can see blue.

God works in believers in two ways. He works externally through the revealed Word; He works internally through the illuminating and convincing Spirit. The majesty of God is in His Word, but we do not see its majesty except the Holy Spirit shows us. Word and Spirit cannot be separated from one another. They are functionally one. The living witness of the Spirit saves the authority of Scripture from "authoritarianism" while the objective truth of the revealed Word saves pretentious men from their own excesses and subjectivity.

The testimony of the Spirit to the truth of the Bible can be established in the hearts of the wise and the unwise, the learned and the ignorant. This testimony does not tell us "how" the Bible is inspired for that can only be ascertained from the Bible's teaching concerning itself, but it does assure the believer that the Bible is, in fact, the inspired Word. This is not, as some have charged, reasoning in a circle. It simply means that God does not separate Word and Spirit. The Bible is self-witnessing. It bears in itself the marks of divine origin which we can plainly see when the Holy Spirit opens the eyes of faith to see them. The fact that doubt and unbelief are due to the sinful condition of man's heart, and not to a deficiency or lack of objective evidence in the Scriptures, can be seen in the fact that the same amount of evidence that may fail to convince a person at one time can later produce a complete conviction when the evidence has been illumined by the Holy Spirit.

THE SPIRIT OF TRUTH

The Christian believes that God is truth because He is the Author of all facts and all meanings. God called the world into existence from "out of nothing," and moment by moment He preserves all that He has created. If we say about reality what God says about it, then we speak the truth. It is that simple. Truth for the Christian means correspondence with the mind of God. If man says that the purpose for his life is to eat, drink, and be merry, he tells the truth only if that is what God says about our purpose.[3]

"But where," one may ask, "is God's mind revealed?" Where do we find God's truth? The answer is simple enough. We find God's truth in Scripture for that is where God has chosen to reveal His person and purpose. The truth that the Holy Spirit, the "Spirit of truth," leads us into is always the truth of the Bible. This is the truth to which the Spirit bears witness. The indwelling

Teacher never teaches man-centered worldly wisdom. He does not even testify to Himself. The Holy Spirit always teaches us to trust in God and His purpose as it is revealed in Jesus Christ. And the only Christ that the Holy Spirit will ever lead us to know is the Jesus Christ whom we know from Holy Scripture.

There is a pagan attitude that has become an accepted philosophy in modern times, sometimes even in the church, that says truth can be determined by its effects on us, that says truth can be known by its practical consequences. This is truth's pragmatic test, and the philosophy that holds to the pragmatic test for truth is called "pragmatism." The touchstone proposition that informs the pragmatic attitude is that knowledge exists for the sake of life, not life for the sake of knowledge. Instead of emphasizing the "content" of knowledge within fixed and unchanging forms, pragmatism offers the practice of knowledge in "the real business of living." Pragmatism stands in opposition to intellectualism and all forms of thinking about absolutes. It is interested only in that which helps one cope with his daily environment, that which helps one get around in the world of his experiences. The only knowledge that matters for the pragmatist is knowledge that makes a difference in our lives. Hence, the pragmatist turns away from abstract ideas and turns toward fruits, consequences, and facts. Ideas are important only as "plans for action." In short, what works is true. It is not the roots of knowledge but the fruits that are important.

Pragmatism is the one major philosophy that has its roots in American soil, and its "results" can be seen in virtually all areas of American life and culture—in education, politics, business, and religion. The pragmatist's concern is for "success." His ethic is the "ethic of success." In the name of results, the pragmatist sacrifices uniqueness and universality. Pragmatic religion becomes a kind of protection that one throws up against the radical demands of biblical faith. Will Herberg, a prominent sociologist and theologian, described the pragmatic attitude toward religion as "a religiousness without religion, a religiousness with almost any kind of content or none, a way of sociability or 'belonging' rather than a way of reorienting life to God." It is, Herberg said, "a religiousness without serious commitment, without real inner conviction, without genuine existential decision. What should reach down to the core of existence, shattering and renewing, merely skims the surface of life, and yet succeeds in generating the sincere feeling of being religious."[4]

Pentecostals hold to a radical Christian commitment and yet they are particularly vulnerable to a pragmatic philosophy, if not in its articulated form, at least to the kind of attitude and ethic that a pragmatic philosophy produces. The Pentecostal movement began as a "life" movement. It has always emphasized "life above knowledge," action, experience, and results. These emphases lend themselves to pragmatism. In proper biblical perspective, all of these emphases have their place. But when Christians allow themselves to be shaped by the mold of worldly thoughts and values, they too become carnal and compromise the integrity of their Christian faith. When Christians accommodate themselves to the pragmatic tenor of culture, they deny the absolute character of biblical truth. The Pentecostal church is today enjoying numerical and financial success. But the church cannot live by pragmatic results alone. It must live in union with its Lord and His purpose. True success always depends upon our living according to God's purpose for our lives. That purpose can only be discovered in the Scriptures. The church's success is always rightly measured by the truth of what God intends the church to be.

Pentecostals must guard against an overly intellectualized faith. Christian faith and worship ought always to be understandable and meaningful for all. And yet Pentecostals must also resist any tendency to become anti-intellectual, to neglect serious study of the Word, or drive a wedge between "life" and "truth." Life that comes from God is always grounded in God's eternal and inmutable truth. God's truth is unique and universal. It is absolute. We cannot adjust God's truth to our interests and purposes. God is not man's "omnipotent servant."

Pragmatic religion is man-centered, not God-centered religion. But it is not our experiences, our actions, our results that are all-important. Christian faith is relevant and practical. God does will for us to be productive and have results. But it must all be on God's terms, according to the Word of truth. Christianity never advocates an attitude that says, "the results justify the means." Workability is not always a sign of truth's presence. Many things will work that are not pleasing to God. This is true, even in the realm of our experiences and emotions. We cannot sanctify or validate an idea or an action simply because we are "blessed" by it. The only criterion by which to judge our ideas, actions, and experiences is the Word of God. The Holy Spirit never condones any other standard of truth.

THE HOLY SPIRIT OUR HELPER

What we have said about the errors of pragmatism should not be construed to mean that Pentecostal religion is removed from life or that it is not interested in practicality and results. To the contrary, Pentecostal religion has always been people-centered. It has always been interested in people's problems, hurts, and needs. The important thing, however, is that human need be understood in the light of the gospel we preach. The work of the Holy Spirit must extend to preaching for it is through preaching that the inner revelation of the Spirit becomes the public property that God intended it to be. Preachers of the Word are God's public servants in making known His holy will to needy, hurting people. There are two ranges of needs that are satisfied by the gospel. There are those needs which are understood by natural reason in light of the human condition. And there are those needs which cannot be perceived in light of the human condition. These needs must be awakened in us by a scriptural understanding of God and ourselves.

Diogenes Allen illustrates this point in *The Reasonableness of Faith* when he reminds us that human need cannot be adequately understood by a simple analysis of the human condition. "That men die is an obvious fact," Allen says, "but that men die because of

God's wrath over their sin is not something which is evident from the fact of death nor from a study of the human condition." That one might escape death, on the other hand, is a distinct hope in men, but the hope which the gospel offers far exceeds the hope that men shall escape death. The gospel promises the penitent and the faithful eternal life as sons and daughters in fellowship with God. To have a strong desire to be good and moral, and then suffer frustration and guilt over one's failure to be so is common to the human condition. Only the gospel can create the yearning for a pure heart and then comfort us with the assurance that Christ's righteousness is now our own.[5]

Nothing is as practical or as relevant to man as the gospel of Christ. It addresses itself to us in such a way as to make our knowledge of God inseparable from a knowledge of ourselves and our needs. It commends itself to us as a solution for our hurts and problems. It meets our needs at the deepest level of human existence. The Holy Spirit inspires the preaching of the gospel for the purpose of revealing a redeeming knowledge of God and ourselves. Wherever the gospel is preached, the Holy Spirit is at work as man's helper.

Before Jesus ascended to heaven, He promised His disciples that they would have the Holy Spirit as a special helper.[6] He promised that the Spirit would come and bear witness to God's gracious work in the hearts of believers. All distinctively Christian experiences that are formed and nourished by the Word of God are the work of the Holy Spirit. He is the One who renews our will, transforms our lives, gives us a sense of forgiveness and acceptance with God, gives us peace, joy in prayer, communion with God, comfort in affliction, a diminished fear of death, the conquest of lustful appetites and passions, the power to resist temptation, development of character and saintliness of life, the strength to undergo self-sacrifice. The testimony of millions, through the ages, has been that the Holy Spirit is their helper. He is the One who has helped Christians cope with life and death. He is the One who is always practical and relevant to human need.

At the point of our extremity, when we do not even know ourselves what we need, the Holy Spirit is there to help us pray according to the will of God. Paul said, "The Spirit helps us in our weakness. We do not know how we ought to pray, but the Spirit himself intercedes for us with groans that words cannot express. And he who searches our hearts knows the mind of the Spirit, because the Spirit intercedes for the saints in accordance with God's will" (Romans 8:26, 27; *NIV)*.

SPIRITUALITY AND SCHOLARSHIP

The Protestant Reformers of the sixteenth century, particularly Luther and Calvin, recognized that one of the gravest errors of the Roman Catholic Church had been to make itself the teacher. By investing all teaching authority in the bishops, Rome depreciated the importance of the Spirit's inner witness and illumination of the Word in individual believers.[7] The Reformers attempted to correct this error by returning to the Holy Spirit as the only true and infallible Teacher. God uses Scripture to make known His will, but it is the Holy Spirit who gives life and meaning to the words. Of all the Reformers, Calvin saw this most clearly:

> As God alone is a sufficient witness of himself in his word, so also the word will never gain credit in the hearts of men, till it be confirmed by the testimony of the Spirit. It is necessary, therefore, that the same Spirit, who spake by the mouths of the prophets, should penetrate into our hearts, to convince us that they faithfully delivered the oracles which were divinely entrusted to them . . . [Scripture] obtains the credit which it deserves with us by the testimony of the Spirit. For though it conciliate our reverence by its internal majesty, it never seriously affects us till it is confirmed by the Spirit in our hearts.[8]

What Calvin had to say concerning the necessary witness of the Spirit to the Word must be understood against the Catholic contention that Scripture is to be received on the basis of the church's authority and interpretation. The church had put itself in the place of the Holy Spirit. This was one side of the error that Calvin and Luther attempted to correct.

There was, however, another side that was equally dangerous. There were the "enthusiasts," the radical reformers, whose extreme emphasis upon the Holy Spirit led them to believe that they had no need of any external authorities or teachers. They did not need the church at all, or even the written Word for they had the Holy Spirit. He was their Teacher. Their claim for "private" interpretation and spiritual guidance led those ultra-protestants to scorn all authorities as well as the need for sound learning and clear doctrine. This was an opposite extreme that the Reformers also stood ready to combat.

The Reformation gave importance to learning and the role of the teacher. But the understanding of that role was greatly modified by Protestant principles. The teacher was no longer regarded as an infallible interpreter, as the teaching magisterium of the Catholic church, but as a learned believer capable of biblical exegesis and an application of the teachings of Scripture. The teacher had no right of "private" interpretation, but rather the duty of constantly reexamining and teaching the church's doctrines. Church teaching and tradition, the Reformers said, must constantly be reexamined in the light of Scripture.

This principle led Protestants to affirm the importance of both sound learning and church councils. The internal witness of the Spirit is not an abandonment of mind or reason. On the contrary, it is through the Holy Spirit that the mind is rationally convinced. This is neither intellectualism nor anti-intellectualism but the necessary union of Word and Spirit. It is important, however, to know what the witness of the Spirit does not mean. It is not the purpose of the Holy Spirit to teach us new truths or propositions. The Spirit illumines and convinces us of the truths that have already been revealed in the Word. But He does not reveal truths that supercede the truth of the Word. If we are to know the truth that God reveals, we must apply ourselves to learning and a knowledge of the Word.

The right and liberty for everyone to interpret and judge is a privilege that is fraught with danger. There is always the danger that fanatical and carnal persons will rise up who presumptuously boast that they know the Spirit's will for the church. To guard against this danger, doctrine must have its public as well as its private test. The public test refers to the common consensus and polity of the church. It is necessary for the faithful to meet together and seek a basis of agreement. This is the purpose for church councils. The wise man Solomon said that "Where no wise direction is, a people falleth, but in the multitude of counsellors there is safety" (Proverbs 11:14). Assemblies of holy men are more than "so many heads, so many opinions." Even in diversity the Holy Spirit can bring forth unity and essential agreement on essential matters.[9]

On sound biblical principles the Protestant Reformers established the following: (1) a healthy regard for the human mind (that is, reason); (2) the importance of education and scholarship; (3) the necessary role that theology must have in the life of the church.

They taught us that Christians must not divorce the heart from the head. God gives us our minds as well as our emotions and our will. We love God with our minds, just as we love God with our hearts. The Christian ought to approach learning and study as an act of worship, humbly bowing the mind before the Author of all truth.

The first characteristic of the Spirit-filled church in Acts that is mentioned is study. Luke tells us that the early Christians "*devoted themselves* to the apostles' teaching," or "to the apostles' doctrine" (Acts 2:42). This was a learning and studying church. "The Holy Spirit had opened a school in Jerusalem," John R. W. Stott says, and "the apostles were the appointed teachers in the school."

The new converts were not enjoying some mystical experience that led them to despise their intellect.

There was no anti-intellectualism. They did not despise the mind. They did not disdain theology, nor did they suppose that instruction was unnecessary. They did not say that because they had received the Holy Spirit, He was the only teacher they needed and they could dispense with human teachers.

Some people today say that, but these early, Spirit-filled Christians did not. They sat at the apostles' feet, they devoted themselves to the apostles' teaching, they were hungry for apostolic instruction. They were eager to learn all they could. They knew Jesus had authorized the apostles to be the infallible teachers of the church, so they submitted to the apostles' authority.[10]

From a New Testament perspective, education and scholarship can never be divorced from true spirituality. Study was the first mark of the Spirit-filled community that Luke mentioned. One of the most important fruits of Pentecost was a devotion to the doctrine of the apostles.

The theological task of the church ought never to be approached as a mere intellectual exercise. The only kind of theological inquiry that can lead to purposeful and spiritual ends is that which is done in an atmosphere of prayer, worship, and openness to the Holy Spirit. After Pentecost the early Church was in a spiritual position to do sound theology because these conditions prevailed. All of the old theology had to be reevaluated in light of the Pentecostal event, and the church could now proceed with the theological task because the Spirit of Truth had been poured out. Pentecostals and Charismatics are experiencing a similar opportunity today. The penetration of Pentecostal power and worship into the structures of older denominations has fomented an unusual amount of inquiry about Pentecostal theology. Many are now interested in a rethinking of the Christian faith that takes a fuller account of the Holy Spirit's person and work. Pentecostals can ill-afford to turn inward, become anti-intellectual, and neglect the necessary role that theology must now serve in the church. There is a greater need than ever before for constructive theology and critical reflection. Pentecostals are more serious about theology and biblical studies than they have ever been. Fully accredited colleges and seminaries, increasing numbers of serious publications, and denominational commitments to the education and enrichment of ministers and laity attest to a new day that has dawned for Pentecostal education.

Numerical growth and financial success have accompanied the pouring out of the Holy Spirit in the twentieth century. The recently published *World Christian Encyclopedia* reports that Pentecostals are now the largest distinct category of Protestants—51 million. It also estimates that there are an additional 11 million Charismatics within the historic denominations. Pentecostals are no longer dismissed as an "across the tracks" phenomena, as they once were.

There is a corresponding responsibility that Pentecostals must now accept. They must speak to the need for a constructive Pentecostal theology as well as self-evaluation. This is not the time for a spirit of triumphalism. Theology is always a matter of self-evaluation. A church committed to responsible theology cannot be interested only in its strengths and the application of its insights to the weaknesses of others; it must ask hard questions of itself. Commitment to Pentecostal power means an ongoing commitment to self-evaluation in the light of God's Word. The prophetic finger of the Church must always be pointed inward as well as outward. A Protestant maxim that Pentecostals must be willing to apply to themselves is *ecclesia reformata sed semper reformanda,* "the church reformed but always to be reformed."

THE HOLY SPIRIT AS DISCIPLER

The purpose of the Holy Spirit is not simply to reveal Christ to us, but to form Christ in us. Discipleship is a matter of spiritual formation. A disciple of Jesus Christ is one who has been totally willed over to Him. A disciple is a learner, a follower, an imitator of Jesus Christ. It means that "we are His"; all of our love, allegiance, and loyalty belong to Him. It involves the setting aside of all other loyalties, comforts, and securities that impede our following in the way of Jesus. Jesus taught that discipleship required self-denial and cross-bearing (Mark 8:34-38; Matthew 10:38-39), a willingness to renounce friends and family (Matthew 10:34-38, 8:18-22; Luke 14:25-33), and giving up everything in order to follow Him (Mark 10:17-22).

A life of discipleship to Jesus Christ cannot be determined by one's own desires or interest. It cannot be determined by loyalty to the community, the family, or denominational affiliation. Discipleship means more than becoming a principled person, an emancipated person, or taking on a new image. In its New Testament usage, the word "disciple" (Greek, *mathetes,* a "learner") implies one who has accepted the mind and life of the teacher. It is the acceptance of Jesus' call and radical obedience to Jesus Christ and His life-view as the central norm of one's life. Discipleship means inclusion in Jesus' death and resurrection; it also means full participation in His vocation. The old self that was crucified with Christ must be willed over to Him again and again (Philippians 3:13; 1 Corinthians 13:8).

Discipleship means being conformed to Christ. He becomes the pattern and the teacher. Christ is our life model. This does not mean that Christ becomes our pattern by being an external authority. Nor does it mean that we become like Christ by acts of slavish imitation. Jesus Christ is our example in that He is God's ideal man. We imitate the quality of Christ's life when we have put on the mind of Christ for the purpose of serving and glorifying God (Philippians 2:1-11; Romans 14:6—15:13). Following Jesus means that we are motivated as Jesus was motivated by the Holy Spirit. It means that the love of God has been poured into our hearts by the Holy Spirit so that we love others as Christ loved us (Romans 5:5). Discipleship is total orientation to God. It is akin to what John Wesley meant by Christian perfection. Writing of perfection, Wesley said:

> In one view, it is purity of intention, dedicating all the life to God. It is giving God all our heart; it is one desire and design ruling all our tempers. It is

the devoting, not a part, but all, our soul, body, and substance to God. In another view, it is all the mind which was in Christ, enabling us to walk as Christ walked. It is the circumcision of the heart from all filthiness, all inward as well as outward pollution. It is a renewal of the heart in the whole image of God, the full likeness of Him that created it. In yet another, it is the loving God with all our heart, and our neighbor as ourselves.[11]

One does not become this kind of disciple by mere discipline or dedication. This can only come through the sanctifying grace of the Holy Spirit. It is only through the Holy Spirit, who is the Spirit of holiness, that we become like Jesus Christ in word and deed. We do what Jesus would do when we have His mind, when we are moved to action by the same Spirit that motivated Jesus' thoughts and actions.

LIBERATED FOR DISCIPLESHIP

Discipleship begins when we are liberated from thoughts and life patterns that bind us to the old life. False needs and securities are oftentimes the greatest hindrances to our becoming Jesus' disciple. The rich young ruler would not follow Jesus because he was bound by his goods. Others would not follow Jesus because they had a greater devotion to father, mother, houses, and lands. Many today are so seduced by affluence and the promise of the "good life" that they find it virtually impossible to be competely willed over to Jesus Christ. Like the rich young ruler, they would like to follow Jesus on their own calculated terms, but they do not find it within themself to forsake their personal wants and satisfactions.

Living as we do in a modern technological society, the temptation to compromise our discipleship to Jesus Christ is compounded by a consumer economy that is forever seeking to create false needs and satisfactions. Many today are literally enslaved by the consumer way of life. Consuming and possessing things becomes the endless and ultimately meaningless round of life. "This spirit of mastery and acquisition," Daniel Migliore says, "is necessarily aggressive because it never finds fulfillment. It drives toward the limitless exploitation of nature and other human beings. Those who are captured by this spirit are themselves dehumanized as well as contributing to the dehumanization of others."[12] Bertrand Russell said that "it is preoccupation with possession more than anything else that prevents men from living freely and nobly."

People become enslaved to a consciousness, created by the devices of advertising, that manipulates them first into wanting things and then buying them. They are deceived into thinking that the things the consumer economy gives them are what they really want—better homes and appliances, faster and more comfortable cars, more leisure and luxury. In effect, most Americans are so completely dominated, brainwashed, and indoctrinated by the propaganda of the advertising media that their desire to consume has become compulsive, irrational, and inhuman. They cannot follow after the quality of Jesus' life and be His disciple because they are bound by false needs and securities.

The way we become captivated by our desire to get and consume was recently illustrated in a story about a group of scientific researchers who needed a rare breed of monkeys for a special research project. They did not know exactly how to catch them in the wild until someone came up with the clever idea of putting fresh smelling peanuts into some longnecked jars. When the monkeys smelled the peanuts they immediately came out of the trees and stuck their hands into the jars. As the scientists approached, the fearful monkeys wanted to flee but in order to do so they had to let go of the peanuts so they could get their hands out of the jars. They were easy prey for the scientists because their desire for peanuts was stronger than their fear of capture. All the scientists had to do was pick up the self-captivated monkeys whose fists were still balled up inside the jars.

The story is a commentary on our modern consumer society. We make monkeys of ourselves, for peanuts, when Jesus Christ would have us follow Him and find our true purpose as sons of God. For freedom, Christ would set us free (Galatians 5:1). But we allow ourselves to be bound by selfish desires and securities. When we allow ourselves to be shaped in the mold of the world, the world puts a monkey on our back. That monkey is our self. Jesus Christ wills to set us free from a self-centered life, free to follow Him and find our true purpose for living.

CONTEMPORARY DISCIPLES

Jesus Christ does not call us to be first century, sixteenth century, or even nineteenth century disciples. Every Christian is called by God to serve his own generation. There is a contemporary history and a contemporary gospel in every generation. The gospel message does not change, but the appropriation of that timeless message to the needs of a changing world is an ongoing operation of the Holy Spirit. When this writer was growing up in a small Pentecostal church, the kind of deliverance deemed necessary for discipleship was usually one that stressed deliverance from the habits and vices that bound so many in that life environment—smoking, drinking, gambling, worldly amusements, and so forth. The life-changing work of the Holy Spirit that one witnessed was beautiful and phenomenal. One witnessed the power of the Spirit that broke the fetters of so many that were bound by bad habits and foul lifestyles and watched as the Holy Spirit bonded these new believers to Jesus Christ.

Many forms of sin that oppress us change very little. But there are others that become a greater threat with changing life conditions so that our discipleship commitments are always being adjusted as we continue to will ourselves over to Jesus Christ amidst those forces that compete for our love and loyalty. Many Pentecostals today face a crisis with regard to their discipleship because they either have not yet understood the commitment that is presently called for or they are not willing to make the radical choices that following Jesus Christ entails.

Contemporary discipleship demands what discipleship has always demanded—a complete willing of oneself over to the way of Jesus Christ. What makes discipleship such an ongoing challenge is the changing conditions under which our faith commitment must be lived out in the world. What is needed is a spirituality that can triumph over the forces that threaten our spiritual integrity today. On the one hand, we need a spiritual integrity that will not be compromised by the ethos of conquest, possession, and consumption that dominates our society. The greatest threat to spiritual integrity today probably lies in a false consciousness of what we really need for a happy and purposeful life. Deliverance from the bondage to false needs and securities is not something we can accomplish ourselves. Those who are dominated by the powers of this world cannot simply free themselves from it.[13] The power of the Holy Spirit is the only power that can free us from the powers that bind us.

The other great need we have is to realize what God frees us for. Discipleship is something very positive. It is a bonding to Jesus Christ and His vision for the world. We need a spirituality that connects us with ever-widening circles of human need and hope. Discipleship does not cut us off from others but moves us away from the old self-enclosed life. We need a spirituality that is inclusive rather than exclusive, active as well as receptive, one that opens us up to the needs of others. This is what the Holy Spirit does. He frees us for fellowship with God and a loving relationship with others. He is the great Discipler for He is the One who frees us from those things that bind us and then bonds us to Jesus Christ and His way of life.

FOOTNOTES

[1]John Calvin, *Commentary on Galatians and Ephesians*, trans. William Pringle (Grand Rapids, Mich.: Eerdman's Publishing Co., 1948), p. 208.

[2]Benjamin Warfield, *Calvin and Augustine* (Philadelphia: Presbyterian and Reformed Pub. Co., 1956), p. 214.

[3]There is an excellent explanation of what truth means, from a

Christian perspective, in Edward Carnell's *Introduction to Christian Apologetics* (Grand Rapids, Michigan: Eerdman's 1948), pp. 45-64.

[4]*Protestant, Catholic, Jew* (Garden City, New York: Doubleday and Co., 1960), p. 260.

[5]Diogenes Allen, *The Reasonableness of Faith*, (Washington, D. C.: Corpus Books, 1968), pp. 53-58.

[6]The Greek word *Parakletos* which is translated "Comforter" in the *King James Version* is derived from *para* meaning "to come to the side of," and *Kaleo* meaning "to call or summons." The word means then "one called to help, aid, advise, or counsel someone."

[7]In Catholicism one was expected to believe what the Church taught, either explicitly or implicitly, as a condition for salvation. Explicit assent meant direct assent to particular propositions. Implicit assent meant that one could simply assent to the teachings of the church. It was not necessary for one to personally know all Catholic truths explicitly, or know the Bible explicitly, but it was expected that one would implicitly accept whatever the church taught.

[8]*Institutes*, I, vii, IV-V.

[9]It is important, I think, for Christians to realize that they do not have to agree on everything. Augustine advised Christians to follow the maxim, "In essentials unity, in non-essentials liberty, in all things charity."

[10]"Setting the Spirit Free," *Christianity Today*, June 12, 1981, p. 18.

[11]*A Plain Account of Christian Perfection*, (London, Epworth Press, 1979), p. 109.

[12]*Called to Freedom*, (Philadelphia: Westminster Press, 1980), p. 88.

[13]Political and economic solutions have been advocated from both the Left and Right. Marxism advocates the destruction of false consciousness through the reevaluation of the society that produces it. The Nazi and neo-Nazi mentality advocates repressive measures. None of these "solutions," however, work. The only true liberation from man's preoccupation with possession is the liberating power of the Holy Spirit who teaches us our true end and purpose.

Chapter 7

The Holy Spirit
and Church Order

One of the results of New Testament scholarship in ecclesiology (that is, the doctrine of the Church) has been the discovery that no distinctive form of church order is prescribed in the New Testament.[1] This finding has had particular value for Christians in the ecumenical movement who find themselves divided over the issue of church order. It is also a significant acknowledgement for Pentecostals whose defense of the charismatic structure of the church has been seriously attacked. More and more scholars and churchmen are now acknowledging what would have been unthinkable just a few years ago. Namely, that the free operation of the Holy Spirit in the church was a prominent feature of New Testament Christianity. What is now being prescribed in many traditional mainline churches is a greater openness to the Holy Spirit. Many are reevaluating their structures and forms of church order in light of a new understanding of the Holy Spirit.

Such acknowledgements ought not to give rise to a wave of triumphalism among Pentecostals in the area of church doctrine, but they are significant. They are significant to Pentecostals because Pentecostals have traditionally been maligned for following a form of church order that scholars have now discovered to be biblically sound. It is also significant because of the admission by those interested in church renewal that Pentecostals have a vital contribution to make.

Catholics, Episcopalians, Presbyterians, Congregationalists, and various free churches have traditionally argued that their church form, or lack of it, was that laid down and prescribed in the New Testament. But except for those scholars whose work in ecclesiology serves a denominational or apologetical function, the current opinion among New Testament scholars is that the church Jesus founded was very different from virtually all church forms that exist today. The new understanding of the church that is emerging is one with a new openness to the Holy Spirit. In fact it is in discussions about the nature of the Church that serious questions about the Holy Spirit have arisen in ecumenical circles. The two are really inseparable. For as one scholar has noted, "Different beliefs about the church are rooted in different beliefs or unbeliefs about the Holy Spirit."[2] What follows is an attempt to describe and evaluate this relationship as it has existed in the major currents of church tradition. Particular attention will be given to the Catholic, mainline Protestant, and Pentecostal/Charismatic understanding of the Holy Spirit as related to church order.

THREE VIEWS OF THE CHURCH

THE EMERGENCE OF ROMAN CATHOLICISM

What happened to the church from the close of the apostolic period until the early third century represents the most drastic change the Christian church has ever undergone. By the opening of the third century, the institutional church had virtually lost its understanding and experience of the vital relationship between the church and the Holy Spirit. The fateful direction which the church took during this period must be understood in light of the efforts it made to repudiate the errors of gnosticism which threatened the integrity of the Christian message and the authority of revealed truth.[3]

Gnosticism was a widespread type of religious thought

and experience in the Graeco-Roman world during the first centuries of the Christian era. Most scholars agree that gnosticism was a loose confluence of diverse streams of thought emanating from pre-Christian mystery religions. Although many mythologies and beliefs informed the movement, there were common motifs among virtually all gnostics. The central conviction was that salvation means the deliverance of the spirit from its imprisonment in the world. This deliverance was believed to occur by means of a secret form of mystical knowledge or gnosis ("gnosis," from which we get the term gnostic, is the greek term for knowledge).

Gnostics were dualists. They regarded the material, physical world as a form of fall from that which is spiritual and good. They commonly spoke of a deliverer who helps release this world's captives by providing them with the secret knowledge that allows them to return to their eternal home of light. Certain gnostics interpreted Christianity in terms of gnostic thought and experience and presented Jesus as a gnostic savior.

Reacting to the gnostic heresy, the post-apostolic church took bold steps to guard against its dangers. Against the gnostic dependence upon secret, mystical forms of knowledge, the church insisted upon the recognition of the teachings of the apostles as the exclusive standard and norm of Christian truth, as the rule of faith. But who would interpret the teachings of the apostles? The church determined that this would be the responsibility of bishops. They were regarded as the rightful heirs and successors of the apostles. Bishops would have teaching authority in the church. These first two steps were taken to counteract the gnostic attempt to establish their own canon of scripture and to provide the church with an objective basis for truth against the gnostic dependence upon secret mystical knowledge reserved for the spiritually elite.

The church took another step, however, that was more radical and erroneous. In response to the gnostic belief in a mystical form of saving knowledge, the church designated itself (the institutional Catholic Church) as the sole channel of divine grace. Over-reacting to the errors of gnosticism, the institutional church found it necessary to reject the belief that the individual could receive saving grace directly from God through the Holy Spirit. It insisted upon membership in the Catholic Church as essential to salvation. The church had received the deposit of truth from Christ, it reasoned, and the Holy Spirit is made available then through the institutional church. The church could now view itself as the ark of salvation, the exclusive channel of divine grace, the only means of salvation. It was only a short step from this position to the view that one is a Christian because he is born to Catholic Christian parents, baptized, and nourished by the sacraments administered by the institutional church.

Augustine, bishop of Hippo in North Africa, defined a sacrament as "a visible sign of an invisible grace." Water is a sign of cleansing; bread is a sign of Christ's body; wine is a sign of His blood. The invisible grace of baptism is cleansing; the invisible grace of the supper is spiritual nourishment. In a sacrament, Augustine taught, the element comes together with the word of promise that is attached to the sign and forms a sacrament. In baptism the water comes together with the promise of forgiveness and the result is baptismal regeneration. The stain of original sin is removed and one enters through baptism into the newness of the Christian life. Since forgiveness is a matter of divine grace, not human choice, a personal decision was not deemed necessary. On this basis the church could justify the baptism of infants. The reception of the Spirit in conversion was no longer viewed by the official church as a matter of personal experience. Spirit-baptism was linked to water baptism. The reception of the Spirit had been reduced to a sacramental occurrence. The person being baptized (usually an infant) was being baptized in order to be saved (baptismal regeneration) instead of being baptized because they had already believed into Christ (believer's baptism).

The Eucharist (that is, the Lord's Supper) was the other sacrament of great importance in the Catholic Church. Through the Eucharist, it was taught, the justifying and sanctifying grace of Jesus Christ is continually being appropriated to the baptized Catholic. Salvation was not taught to be by faith alone but through the sacramental and penitential system of the church. Through the sacraments of the church the remission and forgiveness of post-baptismal sins, and a growth in grace necessary for the final salvation or justification of the believer, was believed to occur. Many sacraments were suggested, but the church eventually settled on seven: baptism, confirmation, eucharist, penance, marriage, ordination, and extreme unction. From the cradle to the grave the Catholic Church attempted to provide its members with sufficient grace.

In Catholicism the "church" always meant the empirical church, the visible institutional church of Rome which saw itself as the dispenser of grace, the place where Christ's presence is celebrated, the possessor of the keys of heaven. Like the garment of Christ, the church was believed to be of one piece. It could not be cut asunder. When schism did occur, as with Luther and the reformers, the Catholic Church could only look upon it as a matter of rending the body. The church saw itself too as a mixed body. The Lord allows the wheat and tares to grow together, allows both good and bad fish in the same net. Separating the true from the false believer can only be an eschatological reality when the Lord of the harvest will make the separation. The real church already exists in the mind of God, composed of those who are predestined (Augustine). Until the Lord of the harvest makes the separation, we should expect the visible church to contain both good and bad.

The hierarchical understanding of the church owed much to the influence of Pseudo-Dionysius in the early middle ages. The institutional church was believed to mirror in its ranks on earth the heavenly realities. On top of the heavenly realities, of course, was the Triune God. At the top of the institutional hierarchy on earth was the pope, the vicar of Christ. Following the pope on a descending scale were the cardinals, archbishops, bishops, priests, and finally the faithful (the recipients of grace). The order and the means of grace moved from the top to the bottom. Everything in the system served to suggest the distinction between the official clergy and the faithful (lay persons). Late in the medieval period the idea emerged that a church council was a better representation of the faithful than the pope (the view of the conciliarists), but it never overcame the earlier emphasis upon papal supremacy and the hierarchical structure of the church. Relying almost exclusively on the pastoral letters and the Acts of the Apostles, where there is a stronger emphasis upon the ministerial office and the role of bishops and church leaders than in other portions of the New Testament, Roman Catholicism has traditionally defended its form of church order on biblical grounds.

The Catholic Church finds its authority in the authority which the apostles received from Christ and transmitted to the hierarchy of the Roman church. The apostles and their successors are what is essential to the Catholic Church. Christ's work is continued in the world through those entrusted with the authority to teach, govern, and perform the sacerdotal duties. While Catholics generally admit that the bearers of apostolic succession have no monopoly on the Holy Spirit, the gifts and ministry of the church traditionally have been understood to rest with the official clergy. This has resulted in a special class of those believed to be endowed with gifts and an unbiblical distinction between clergy and laity. Hans Küng, a contemporary Catholic who is critical of the structure of his own church, reminds Catholics that "God has not only placed apostles in the church, but prophets and teachers, miracles, gifts of healing, services of help, power of administration, and the speaking of various tongues . . ."[4] Fom a New Testament perspective, it is impossible to limit the Charisma (gifts) of the Holy Spirit to officeholders. All who receive the Holy Spirit are empowered and impelled by Him to witness of the risen Lord and to continue His work in the world through the power of His gifts.

The error in the Catholic understanding of the church is in its belief that the work of the Holy Spirit has passed into the life and work of the church so that the church now performs the functions of the Holy Spirit. The Holy Spirit is restricted within the institutional and sacramental structures of the church. Christ is extended in the world through the institutional body more so than through His dynamic presence and work in the life of individual believers.[5] The Holy Spirit is thought of more as a channel, an impersonal principle, through which the church carries out its work. His person and lordship over the church is not adequately acknowledged. The gift of the Spirit and the charisms are canalized in the historical body, but they are not allowed full exercise in the structures of the church. Since Vatican II in the 1960s when the doors of the church were left ajar and the subsequent penetration of the Holy Spirit occurred, the Catholic Church has experienced charismatic renewal in many quarters. But it remains to be seen what God would do if only the Holy Spirit were allowed to confront and guide the church as a living power and presence.

THE PROTESTANT UNDERSTANDING OF THE CHURCH

Following the lead of Luther and Calvin, Protestants have been critical of Rome's identification of the gospel with what is spoken by the institutional church. Whereas Catholicism understands God to be present to His people through the church, Protestants understand God to be present through the Word and sacraments of the gospel. The heart of the reformer's protest was their belief that the Roman church had made itself Christ and in doing so had become anti-Christ. What the reformers wanted most was to reestablish the sovereignty of Christ over His Church.

The centrality of the gospel was the glory of reformation theology. "Wherever," said Luther, "you see this Word preached, believed, confessed, and acted on, there do not doubt that there must be a true holy catholic church . . . for God's Word does not go away empty."[6] Calvin similarly wrote: "Wherever we see the Word of God sincerely preached and heard, wherever we see the sacraments administered according to the institution of Christ, there we cannot have any doubt that the Church of God has some existence, since His promise cannot fail, 'Where two or three are gathered together in my name, there am I in the midst of them.' "[7]

The reformers made the gospel of Christ central to everything else. They aimed to reform the old church by the Word of God. The church was to be captive to God's Word. Nothing adorns the Protestant heritage more brilliantly than the twin principles of *sola Scriptura* (Scripture alone) and *sola gratia* (grace alone).

Catholicism assented to the principle of salvation by divine grace, but the principle had been overlaid by the "merit of good works" (religious and ascetic practices, reverence for relics, pilgrimages to shrines, indulgences, and so forth). The reformers were moved by a strong revulsion against all this. They embraced the biblical teaching of justification by grace alone as taught by Paul and later elaborated by Augustine of Hippo. In his exposition on the sacraments and the doctrine of the church, Augustine stood squarely in the Catholic tradition. He was himself a bishop. But in his teachings on grace, Augustine differed from much of the Catholic tradition. The reformers looked upon the doctor of grace as their own champion.

Augustine placed the total responsibility for man's salvation upon the initiative of God's gracious election. In the mysterious but allwise counsel of God some are chosen for salvation; others are destined for perdition. That which saves is the word of promise, the word of grace and forgiveness which stems from eternal predestination. Both Luther and Calvin followed Augustine in his emphasis upon God's gracious action. But they differed with the Catholic conception of sacramental grace.

First, the Protestants reduced the number of sacraments from seven to two: water baptism and the Lord's Supper. These were the only two that were believed to have been instituted by Christ. Their understanding of a sacrament also differed from the common Catholic conception. A sacrament does not work grace; it is a means that God uses to make grace available to us. The grace that God communicates through the sacrament is the grace God provides because of the word of promise.

Calvin defined a sacrament as, "An outward sign by which the Lord seals on our consciences the promises of his good will toward us."[8] What validates a sacrament is the gracious promise of the covenant that is appropriated to us through faith by the Holy Spirit. The Word and the Spirit are inseparable.

The reformers changed the sacramental understanding of the church. But just as importantly, they removed the hierarchy from the church and replaced the sacerdotal "office" of the priest with the concept of the "priesthood of all believers." Every Christian is a priest and can preach the word and administer the sacraments. For the sake of church order, Protestant congregations call gifted men and women to fill the offices of the church and see that they are properly trained for their task. But ordination has no sacramental meaning or exalted status in the Protestant tradition. The minister is a servant of the Word he proclaims. His primary responsibilities are to preach the Word and administer the sacraments. The minister's effectiveness and success do not depend upon personal gifts or charisma but the faithfulness of God to His covenant promise. The congregation is reminded of God's faithfulness through the sacraments of Baptism and the Supper. When the minister proclaims the Word of promise and administers the sacraments, he does not stand above the people but with them. He opens the Word of God so that it may be clearer for all to hear and understand.

THE CHARISMATIC STRUCTURE OF THE CHURCH

Roman Catholicism stresses the centrality of the church in its institutional form. It believes that the institutional Roman Church is the extension of Christ's incarnation. It teaches that the church is a mediator between God and man in matters of salvation and the means whereby Christ is made present to His people through the sacraments.

Protestants, on the other hand, stress the message of the church. They understand the church to be a fellowship of believers, the mystical body of Christ, the organic union of all who are spiritually joined to Christ. The saving work of Jesus Christ is appropriated through the Holy Spirit. Christ is made present to His people through the Word and sacraments of the gospel. But the preaching of the gospel is central. The rediscovery of the gospel (that is, the "good news" of God's graciousness in Jesus Christ) and a renewed emphasis upon the authority of the Word are hallmarks of Protestantism. All Protestants can be proud of their Word-centered heritage.

Many Protestant scholars now admit, however, that there are serious deficiencies in the mainline Protestant understanding of the Church. The Reformers (Luther and Calvin) taught that the Church exists where the Word is truly preached and the sacraments rightly administered. The effect which this emphasis had was to overly intellectualize the meaning of faith. Leslie Newbigin, former bishop in the Church of Scotland, underscored this point when he wrote that traditionally, "The church has been more concerned with correct doctrine and correct administration than with the character of the church as a community of faith in which the Holy Spirit is recognizably present with power."[9] What Newbigin suggests is that Catholicism is primarily concerned with the church's *structure*, Protestants with its *message*, but that neither stress the *life* of the church which is the Holy Spirit. Though light and life can never really be separated, what is most conspicuously absent in the church today is life.

H. Wheeler Robinson, a leader and scholar in the Christian church, tells how that during a serious illness he was brought to ask himself why the truths of "evangelical" Christianity which he had preached to others now failed to bring him personal strength. "They seemed true," he said, "but they lacked vitality. They seemed to demand an active effort of faith, for which the physical energy was lacking. The figure that presented itself . . . was that of a great balloon, with ample lifting power—if only one had the strength to grasp the rope that railed down from it." The result of this experience, Robinson reports, was that it led him to seek for what was missing in his own conception of evangelical truth. "I found it," he confessed, "in the relative neglect of the Holy Spirit in which the New Testament is so rich."[10] From this experience, Dr. Robinson was spurred into a fifteen-year study of the Holy Spirit which resulted in one of the most fruitful studies to date on the subject which he entitled *The Christian Experience of the Holy Spirit.*

Clark Pinnock, noted evangelical Baptist theologian, recently made a similar observation. "It is not a new doctrine we lack. What we need is a new dynamism that will make all of the old evangelical convictions operational," Pinnock stated. "We need not so much to be educated as to be vitalized. It is not a doctrine of the Spirit that we need but a movement of the Spirit, pervading and filling us, setting our convictions on fire."[11]

It is not enough for the church to have the truth on ice. The truth of the gospel needs always to be aflame by the presence and power of the Holy Spirit. In his work on *Church Order in the New Testament,* Edward Schweizer concludes that for the contemporary church to be successful where it lives it must live out of God's freedom and faithfulness and not out of its own order or religious vitality.[12] The New Testament pattern for church order calls for a church that is open and desirous of the gifted ministry of the Holy Spirit. The church cannot be true to itself or its Lord when its order does not reflect an openness to the Holy Spirit's freedom to work in and through the members of the body. This is the one thing necessary in order for the church to be structured charismatically.

The term "charisma" is a word that carries many meanings in popular speech. It may refer to unusual facets of human personality. But this is not the sense in which we are using the term. In contemporary religious usage the term is often used as a synonym for neo-Pentecostal or the so-called Charismatic movement. But neither is this the sense in which we are using the term. The term has a New Testament usage. Charismatic, in a New Testament context, refers to the endowments or gifts with which the Holy Spirit enriches and equips the church for service. The gifts, or *charismata,* have their origin in the gracious (Greek *charis*, "grace") operation of the Holy Spirit, and they are bestowed in order to equip God's people for work in His service (Ephesians 4:12). It is important to understand that Charismatic gifts do not refer only to the more spectacular gifts of the Holy Spirit. They refer to all of the Holy Spirit's gifts for ministry.

The term "Charismatic" ought not to be used then as an existentially laden concept devoid of biblical content and/or structure. We have been careful to retain the word "structure" in our indicated need for the continuance of God's gracious gifts in the church. This is a matter of no small significance, for many tend to think of the church as a free-floating enterprise operating within some kind of twilight zone. Just as the *Logos* took on human form in Jesus Christ, the church needs some structural form through which Christ's work can be extended in the world through the power of the Holy Spirit. The church must have a recognizable shape that facilitates its mission. The enduring insight of Roman Catholicism is its recognition that the body of Christ is meant to be visibly and universally extended in the world. Its enduring error has been its tendency to identify the structures of the Roman church with the incarnate Christ. Christ's body can, in reality, only be extended in the world through the Holy Spirit. He alone can represent Christ. Through the Holy Spirit, Christ is represented so that the church can know Him and draw from Him its life. Jesus Christ is the vine; we are the branches. The life in the body comes from Him. Without Him, we can do nothing (John chapter 15). It is only through the Holy Spirit tht Christ is made present and real to us.

It is not that the church cannot be an institution, but to prevent it from being only an institution we must stress the church's need for a continual openness to the Holy Spirit. The historical pattern has been for the church to settle down in established forms, to give these forms instrinsic value, and to resist any disturbing of the structures. Established churches historically have curtailed and even opposed the operation of certain of the Holy Spirit's gifts. Churches too often mistrust the free operation of God's Spirit. Only infrequently does one find mainline churches that are trustful enough of the Holy Spirit to allow Him to blow where He wills without official permission.

Church structures are necessary. They have a positive value and good because they reflect something essential to our understanding of God; namely, His faithfulness. Order in the church bespeaks the continuity of God's grace and His faithfulness to His people. God's steadfastness *(hesed)* remains when all else seems chaotic and uncertain. When the church gathers to hear the Word of God and to worship, it ought to be reminded of God's steadfast love in the order and structures of the church. Church structure, like creeds, gives shape to one's faith. Our life together within the trusting community always needs a shape, a morphology. The point is not that our faith does not need the structures of the church but that the structures themselves ought to reflect the church's origin and destiny as a pilgrim people. Church structures ought never to obscure or obstruct the church's purpose.

Commitment to charismatic structures in the church is nothing more nor less than an openness to and a desire for the free gifts of the Lord of the Church whose Spirit is the Church's life. It has nothing to do with the endorsement or rejection of a religious movement, a particular style of worship, or a charismatic type of leadership. Worship is the life of the church. Through its worship the church witnesses to the resurrected Lord who lives in the church through the Holy Spirit. True worship is itself inspired by the Spirit of God. Where the church is structured charismatically, the people of God are encouraged to worship both in Spirit and in truth (John 4:24).

Church order should allow for and encourage expression by the body. It ought never to become a negative expression for doing things "decently and in order." Yet, worship ought not to become so privitized that the corporate nature of the body is forgotten or neglected. The richness of the variety in the church stems from its individual members who have unique needs and distinctive gifts. Too little attention to the needs and contributions of its individual members make one's understanding of the body spurious and superficial, but too much emphasis upon individual-"ism" and free expression can make a mockery and abuse of the church's corporate nature.

The church is communal in its essence, but the communal relation is somewhat analogous to Christian marriage. A marriage involves individual members, but they live together as a unit. In the body of Christ individual members live together in relation to God and each other through the Holy Spirit. Human relations alone never constitute the church. Jesus Christ is the necessary relation which brings and holds Christians together. The Christian community is a spiritual reality because it is founded in and lives through the life of Jesus Christ. It does not live by the values and loyalties of the world but by its own law of life, Christian love (agape). Love manifests itself in service (diakonia), the only office in the church to which all Christians are called. If anyone desires an office in the church, let him serve. Whatever gifts or ministry one may have, that which is necessary to the upbuilding of the body is a willingness to serve others. Humility and service are the marks of greatness in God's kingdom. The church has Jesus for its model, "Who, though he was in the form of God [preexistent and divine], did not count equality with God a thing to be grasped, but emptied himself, taking the form of a servant, being born in the likeness of men" (Philippians 2:5-7, RSV).

A commitment to charismatic structures is a commitment on the part of the visible church to organize itself so that it can more effectively serve as Jesus served in the power of the Holy Spirit. The church cannot be an extension of Christ in any other way. That which is not inspired by the Holy Spirit can be nothing more than the work of the flesh.

THE SHAPE OF THE CHURCH

THE LORDSHIP OF JESUS CHRIST

What would be the shape of a church with charismatic structures today? If we are to talk seriously about such a church, we ought to be able to say something about its morphology. The point of what we have been saying is that when the church's vision is clear, when it is motivated, renewed, and equipped for service by the Holy Spirit, its outward shape will be susceptible to change. It is not the outward form of the church that is so important. What is important is that the church remain faithful to its Lord and to the task it has been given. If it is truly led and empowered by the Holy Spirit, the structures it assumes will give witness to its true nature and task.

The controlling principle of the church must always be the lordship of Jesus Christ. Nothing about the church is meaningful apart from its Lord. Whatever shape the church takes, it must resemble Jesus Christ. He is the living reality that gives purpose and life to the church. When the early church expressed its deepest conviction regarding Jesus Christ, it came in the form of a confession that, "Jesus is Lord."

When Christians make that confession today, they are making the most profound confession about the church. They are confessing that Jesus Christ is the reality made present to us now in fellowship and worship through the Holy Spirit. Our confessions, however, find meaning only through what we practice. Our actions reflect what we have truly confessed in our hearts. If Jesus is really Lord, it will be seen in His effect upon our life.

Jesus Christ is the model for the church. If He is Lord, the church's life and purpose will take on the shape of Jesus' ministry. Its vocation will conform to His. One naturally asks, "What was Jesus' vocation?" "How does Jesus' model set the agenda for the church's work in the world today?"

It is shocking and sometimes disturbing when we

first discover that Jesus never spoke of the church as
an institution such as later developed in Christendom.
Jesus did not really come to establish an institution as
much as He did to establish a new set of relationships.
The kingdom of God was Jesus' central message. Those
who are born into this Kingdom through the Spirit
participate in its life and relationships and move together
toward the consummation of this age as a pilgrim
people. It was inevitable that the pilgrim community
would organize itself and take on an institutional form
in order to facilitate its task. As the historic church
grew in numbers and its organizational life became
more complex, its needs for an institutional form became
more evident. Organizational structure is evident in the
New Testament itself, as the Jerusalem Council (Acts
15) and the pastoral Epistles attest. The danger which
organization and institutional structures posed for Kingdom life lay not in the structures themselves. They
could serve an instrumental good. The danger lay in the
human propensity to depend upon the power of organization and the forms of life it generates. The tendency is
for structures to become impersonal, bureaucratic, and
competitive. Life together in the body of Christ was
never meant to be lived according to such secular forms.
The church was not meant to be modeled after giant
business corporations, organized for efficiency and profit,
any more than its early form was meant to be modeled
after the organizational structures of the ancient Roman
Empire.

When the church shapes itself after the model of
secular structures, it takes on their social ethic. It sells
itself to an empty concept. As William Whyte wrote in
The Organization Man, the social ethic that informs
modern-day organization life elicits more than one's
labor and sweat. It demands one's loyalties, one's soul.
Organizational life creates a climate that inhibits initiative and change. It demands adjustment to the organization and cooperation from all concerned, but it fosters a
wrong basis for them. One is asked to cooperate for no
real reason or rationale other than group harmony. One
may be led to believe that his interests are being pro-

tected when really the organization is looking only to the organization's interests and values. People tend to be valued for their loyalty to the organization. Leaders are reduced to managers. Principles of modern management become more highly valued than leading by example. The Christian who allows the organization ethic to be his judge ultimately sacrifices himself on the altar of the idea that the interest of the organization and the kingdom of God are wholly compatible.

Secular forms of organization life are generally static, not dynamic. They may even cling to known disadvantages rather than risk change. Organizational life is pragmatic and utilitarian. Thought and action become hostages to prevailing opinion. One comes to feel more like an object being acted upon than an acting subject. The psychological result is likely to be a loss of initiative and low self-esteem.

This is not life together in the body as Christ intended. The church of the living God cannot model itself after secular forms of organizational life. Christ's purpose was to form a community of loving, caring, and serving believers. He came to give us dignity and purpose as sons of God. The so-called "spiritual church" and the "organized church" always need each other. They cannot be separated, but they ought not to be confused. The former provides vision and inspiration; the latter provides the vehicle through which the purpose and ideal of the spiritual church finds expression. The organized church must be constantly renewed. For only as it finds constant renewal through the living Christ can it maintain its vision and fulfill its purpose. Loss of meaning and purpose always characterize the church when it has lost contact with its spiritual center.

The Holy Spirit is an eternal contemporary to all those whose lives are centered in Jesus Christ. It is the Holy Spirit who is permanent, not the institutions and instruments which He chooses to use. The only enduring truth is the truth of all that of which Christ is the center. This truth is not to be found through separation from the organized church but through a renewed vision of what the organized church was meant to be.

The church ought not to settle down into forms which restrict its life. It must always remember its vocation as a pilgrim people. When the church organizes itself, it does so for the purpose of making progress toward its goal—not for the purpose of settling down.

Jesus' vocation was to reconstitute the nation of Israel according to the terms of the new covenant. His aim was not to sanctify and perpetuate Jewish institutions and customs but to lead the chosen people into a new covenant relationship with God through the Spirit. The reconstitution of Israel, symbolized by the twelve apostles, was to be one of right relationships, of persons in right relationship with God and with one another. These relationships could not be facilitated by custom and institutional order as they could by the free movement of the Holy Spirit in the lives of God's people.

Jesus showed no particular disdain for fixed structures except when such forms and customs inhibited the realization of covenant relations. But clashes inevitably arose when the Jews saw that Jesus' teachings, if followed, would change the established customs and institutional life of Israel. Instead of outward ceremonial cleansing and external displays of righteousness, Jesus taught purity of heart and justice toward one's neighbor (Mark 7:18, 19; Matthew 23:25, 26; Luke 11:39-41).

Institutions and customs are not easily changed. Those who advocate change are always suspect in the eyes of those for whom old ways have become sacrosanct. It is not an insignificant fact that the first Christian martyr was one who advocated a change in attitude toward Jewish customs and institutions. Stephen saw more clearly than most that Jesus' teachings and example, if followed, would change Jewish customs. He accused the Jews of being a stiff-necked people, set in their ways. For his charges against the Jews, and the pilgrim mentality which he espoused, Stephen was stoned to death by an angry Jewish mob (Acts chapter 6 and 7). Like Jesus, Stephen was charged with speaking against the Temple, the Law, and the customs of Moses (Acts 6:13, 14).

Stephen taught that the way of Christ is like a

journey. The journey began with Abraham's call out of Mesopotamia into a promised land. The sojourn continued for the covenant people with Joseph's journey into Egypt and the Hebrew's deliverance out of that land by Moses some 400 years later. God's dwelling place during the time of deliverance was a portable tent. Solomon later built a permanent house (Temple) for Yahweh, and the Jews began the process of institutionalizing their God. When Stephen insisted that the Lord God could not be made to dwell in houses or be contained within human structures or institutions, it was more than the angry mob could stand. Stephen's sermon drove the Jews to madness, and they stoned him for proclaiming the message that God's purpose in Jesus Christ was not to establish and perpetuate human institutions but to establish a relationship of love between God and man and between every man and his neighbor. Human institutions are useful and good to the extent that they further the relationships made possible through the death and resurrection of Jesus Christ. When they hinder these relationships, they lose their value.

God's vessels are earthen. Heavenly treasure may be manifested in them but never fully contained. The life which comes from God ought never to be confused with the forms through which it is manifested. When Jesus is truly Lord, the church will resemble Him in its life and its form. The shape of the church will be Christlike.

THE RE-PRESENTATION OF JESUS CHRIST THROUGH THE HOLY SPIRIT

The common life which we enjoy in the body of Christ is made possible through Jesus' death and resurrection. The richness of relationships in the body would not be possible apart from Jesus Christ, the Lord of the Church.

In the economy of grace God has willed to impart Christ's life and form to us through the Holy Spirit. The Holy Spirit is the Life-Giver, the One who represents Jesus Christ in the Church.

In Catholic understanding, Christ is made present through the sacraments of the Church. In mainline

Protestantism God is said to be present to the people through the Word and sacraments of the gospel. Pentecostal theology does not differ in its teaching that the gospel of Christ is central. The church, the Word, and the sacraments are all instruments of the Spirit. Word and Spirit always belong together. The Holy Spirit never contradicts nor contravenes the Word. What makes the Pentecostal message different is not a lessening in importance of the church, the sacraments, or the Word. The difference lies in the Pentecostal emphasis upon the Holy Spirit as the One who re-presents Jesus Christ in the Church. The church can only know and experience the living Christ through the Holy Spirit who re-presents him.

The truth revealed in Christ admits of no external proof until it has been made the inward possession of the believing mind by the convincing power of the Holy Spirit. Christian faith cannot be created by dogma or the church. Without the Holy Spirit, instruments are mere instruments. They lack the life and power which make them living and transforming realities. God's revelation of Himself comes only through the Holy Spirit. Until the truth of Jesus Christ is attested to the soul by God's Spirit, there can be no real change in conviction or behavior. The only sufficient witness to God is God himself. When we are brought face to face with God through the Holy Spirit, the Christian religion begins to live. The Spirit prompts a response of the mind and heart to the Word. Beliefs become personal beliefs. Actions become responsible, Spirit-prompted actions. Lives become filled with meaning and life.

When the church becomes a living reality, convinced of Christian truth in heart and mind, inspired to worship, and equipped to proclaim Christ by the power of the Holy Spirit, it becomes a charismatic community. Its structures reflect both the freedom of the Spirit's action and the church's conviction that God's grace in Jesus Christ is continuous and faithful. When the Church hears the Word of God, it is reminded of God's faithfulness to His promises. When it breaks the bread and drinks from the cup, it remembers again the continuity of His grace.

In a charismatic community the gifts cannot be separated from the Giver. Jesus Christ is the Giver of gifts (Ephesians 4:7-13). He gives the church all that is necessary to its life and its mission in giving the Holy Spirit. The purpose of spiritual gifts is to honor and exalt the Giver, not the recipient. God honors those who honor Christ. When Christ is exalted, the church is built up.

Gifts ought never to become objects of pride. When they do, the individual is exalted, and division occurs in the body. Every member in the body should exercise the gift that has been given to him or her by the Holy Spirit for the upbuilding of the whole body (Romans chapter 12). The completeness of the body depends upon the participation of every member. The unity of the body depends upon every member's selfless consideration of others. W. J. Hollenweger has beautifully stated the principle: "The individual does not make his gift the measure for others but the others become the measure for the exercise of his gift."[13]

There is certainly a need and a place for the more extraordinary gifts in the church. But these should not be emphasized at the expense of the less conspicuous gifts which are just as important and necessary for the proper functioning of the church. An examination of Paul's lists of spiritual gifts reveal that the Holy Spirit has varied the gifts in order to serve the total need of the church. Spiritual gifts are related to such diverse tasks as preaching, giving, teaching, administration, helps, and so forth (1 Corinthians 12:38-31; Romans 12:6-8; Ephesians 4:11). The importance of spiritual gifts lies not in their miraculous quality or unusual form of manifestation, but in their responsible place in the church so that the whole body may be built up and equipped for service (1 Corinthians 12:7).

The charismata are not limited to a special class or rank of Christians. All Christians are gifted by the Holy Spirit. The priesthood of all believers should be much in evidence whenever the church is structured charismatically. The church ought never to be structured so as to exclude any of the people of God (the *laos)* from meaningful participation. Charismata are not limited to the clergy, administrators, or office-holders. Leadership is necessary in the church. The Holy Spirit gifts men and women for that function. But He does not gift some for the purpose of creating a leading class to dominate the body. The mark of spiritual leadership is service *(diakonia),* not domination.

Finally, spiritual gifts ought never to be exercised contrary to the instruction of the Word. Every gift has its counterfeit. The only safeguard against error is truth. God's Word is truth. Whatever lays claim to one's trust and obedience as a spiritual reality has for its judge the Word of God. We are to "test the spirits to see whether they are of God" (1 John 4:1, *RSV).* The church is a pneumatic reality (1 Corinthians 3:16; Ephesians 2:22; 1 Peter 2:5), but it is a spiritual reality built upon the authoritative witness of the prophets and apostles. The Church is likened to a spiritual building, a temple for the habitation of God through the Spirit (Ephesians 2:19-22). Jesus Christ is the cornerstone of the building. When the church is founded upon Him, it is like a house that is built upon a rock that cannot be moved or eroded by the floods of error and evil that assault it (Luke 6:18).

THE CHURCH AS AN ESCHATOLOGICAL REALITY

The church is an eschatological reality. It has been on pilgrimage since Abraham was called out of Ur, and it will remain on pilgrimage until the coming of its Lord. The church exists in the tension between the "already" and the "not yet." The time of the church is now because it is indwelt by the Holy Spirit. The Holy Spirit is the firstfruits of that future glory which is not yet but which will be fully realized when Christ returns (Romans 8:23). The Holy Spirit, which the church has already received, is the first installment of that which is to come (2 Corinthians 1:22; 5:5).

Amidst earthly trials and obstacles, the church remains

militant—overcoming the forces arrayed against it and remaining faithful to its task. Its place of responsibility is the world. The church is the extension of the incarnate Christ, continuing Christ's ministry in the power of the Holy Spirit. Its duties in the world cannot be shirked. Yet, the church is not to take on a secular form in order to accomplish its end. God calls a people out of the world and equips them with the Holy Spirit so that they can be sent back into the world for the purpose of continuing Christ's vocation. The church must not be afraid to get its hands dirty. It should accept its mundane tasks cheerfully, without any sense of self-righteousness or moral superiority. The kingdom of Christ, which is not of this world, is best reflected when the church has its own internal relations and sense of mission in order. The church is called upon to reflect that toward which it is moving as a pilgrim people.

The life of the church is to be determined by its end. It does not have to be determined by present circumstances. Early Christians found that they could rejoice in the midst of trials and suffering because the power of the Age to Come already possessed them. When the church is indwelt by the Holy Spirit, it gives witness to the end toward which it is moving. Its structures, as well as its life, testify to that which is coming to meet it.

The church must avoid the temptation to become preoccupied with itself. It has not been commissioned for the purpose of making itself an end. When it does, it turns inward, becomes self-centered, and treats the world indifferently. As Daniel Jenkins has rightly stated, "The wilderness through which we pass must not be treated with indifference . . . we must claim as much of the world for the Kingdom as we can. We are colonists of heaven as well as a pilgrim people. We have a responsibility to refashion as much of the world as we can after the likeness of our homeland. We are a people 'called out' for others."[14]

The church has then a twofold responsibility: to be faithful to its message and to model that message for those whom the message is intended. A church that turns inward and becomes obsessed with preserving its own heritage and structures can too easily become its own idol. A one-generation model of the church is to be preferred over one that fixates on itself.

Even the impermanent nature of the charismata (spiritual gifts) attests to the eschatological movement of the church. They too lie between the "already" and the "not yet." Their operation belongs to the imperfections of this passing age, as the experience of the Corinthian Christians graphically attests. "When that which is perfect has come," Paul said, "that which is imperfect will be done away with" (1 Corinthians 13:10). Excesses and disorder connected with the operation of spiritual gifts in the church are to be expected amid the imperfections of the church in the realm of the "not yet." When disorder occurs or the church loses sight of the real purpose of spiritual gifts, it ought to be corrected in the light of scriptural teaching (1 Corinthians chapters 12-14 and Ephesians chapter 4). But the Church of Jesus Christ ought always to avoid the temptation to prescribe and control the Spirit's movement because it fears imperfection and disorder. The need for scriptural regulation has been unjustifiably used by many as an excuse for repression and a denial of the need for unusual operations of the Holy Spirit in the church today. The imperfections of the present age will only be fully corrected in the consummation. The fact that scriptural teaching and regulation is provided is itself implicit scriptural approval of the Spirit's operation in the pilgrim church. One does not regulate that which is unwarranted. If it is not needful, it is abolished. God's purpose does not call for the abolition of Charismatic activity in an imperfect church. It calls for scriptural guidance as the pilgrim church makes its way through the wilderness of this imperfect age.

As Hollis Gause explains, "The very existence of rules of government for the ministries of the Holy Spirit is tacit approval of their operation."

> Paul's instructions on the control of the spiritual gifts presupposes their legitimacy. To find in rules of operation a prohibition of existence is to reveal one's own prejudices. What is aberrational or spe-

cial to a unique situation is not understood as normative; hence, there is no expectation of its continuing regularity in the church. By the Pentecostal presupposition those things that are regulated and hence normative may be expected as regularly continuing in the life of the church. Hence, they may take on a doctrinal significance.[15]

FORM FOLLOWS FUNCTION

In *Frontiers for the Church Today* Robert McAfee Brown compares the adjustment in modern day ecclesiology with the Copernican revolution of the seventeenth century which required one of the greatest mental adjustments that human kind has ever been called upon to make. It required men to recognize that the sun, rather than the earth, is the center of the solar system. In the twentieth century, Albert Einstein challenged another old assumption when he suggested that space and time are not absolutes but that they are relative to the frame of reference of a particular observer.

The church, like any establishment, has always found it difficult to come to terms with ideas that challenge old assumptions. Religious establishments have found it particularly difficult to make the kingdom of God, rather than the institutional church, the center. And, they have not looked kindly on those who suggest that the church's structures and forms of order may not be as "absolute" as before assumed.

Slowly but surely the church is realizing in our day that its structures are not what is central. The value of structures can only be determined in light of what God wills to accomplish through them in any given time or place. The recognition of this fact has been an ecclesiastical counterpart to the Copernican and Einsteinian revolution in science.

A basic law of architecture is that form follows function. An architect does not build a structure and then ask if it can be put to use. An architect is commissioned to create forms and structures that will serve a purpose.

Similarly, Christians ought not to create a series of

institutional structures and then ask "how" or "for what purpose" they can be put to use. The form which the church assumes ought to be determined by the church's function.[16] The primary obligation of the church is always to its present generation. When the church's vision is clear concerning its function, it can then proceed to establish the forms that will facilitate its task. As the church seeks to be true to its dual task of being faithful to its own purpose and speaking relevantly to its own times, it will discover that from one time and place to another its forms may have to be altered or replaced altogether. Particular structures and forms of order may be expendable.

The one thing about which we can be sure, however, is that it will always be necessary for the church to assume some shape or form. Christianity is not a formless faith. But the form which the church assumes must be one that facilitates the free movement of the Holy Spirit. Its structures must be charismatic structures. By the same token it must be remembered that Christianity is a catholic (universal) and communal faith. The structures and forms of the church always need to reflect a sense of continuity within the body of Christ. Christians will always need to gather together so that the grace and truth of the past may be reappropriated for the present. The particular manner in which the church gathers and scatters will undoubtedly change with human conditions. The important thing is that the church's form of order and its structures be consistent with the message that it communicates.

The truth of the Christian faith was communicated to humankind through the incarnate Christ. He is the church's indispensable message and the form to which the church is called to conform. God's love for the human family was not expressed through some "spiritual" disembodied truth. It was made manifest in human form. As the church takes up Christ's ministry of reconciliation, through the power of the Holy Spirit, it too will minister to human need under human conditions. But it will do so as a pilgrim people. It must be careful not to become so encumbered by its own heavy baggage that it compromises its own usefulness and purpose. The church must learn to travel light.

FOOTNOTES

[1] Among others, Eduard Schweizer, Colin Williams, Adoph Martin Ritter, and Ernst Käsemann acknowledge the ecclesiological pluralism of the New Testament. See, for example, Käsemann's "Unity and Multiplicity in the New Testament Doctrine of the Church," in *Questions.*

[2] George S, Hendry, *The Holy Spirit in Christian Theology* (London: SCM, 1957), p. 53.

[3] The most illuminating account I have read of the direction which the Christian church took in reponse to gnosticism in the second century is A. C. McGiffert's *Primitive And Catholic Christianity,* An Address Delivered on the Ocasion of His Induction into the Washburn Professorship of Church History in Union Theological Seminary, New York (New York: John C.Rankin Co., Printers, 1893). The point that McGiffert makes in the address is that by the beginning of the third century the spirit of primitive Christianity, which was based on the felt presence and miraculous working of the Holy Spirit in the church, had virtually disappeared.

Adolf Harnack says practically the same thing. He says that Christianity came into being as "the religion of the Spirit and power" and only lost this character and became the religion of form and order toward the end of the second century *(The Expansion of Christianity in the First Three Centuries,* E. T. I., pp. 250 ff.).

[4] Hans Küng, "The Charismatic Structure of the Church," *The Church and Ecumenism* (New York: Paulist Press), p. 55.

[5] For a fuller criticism of the Roman Catholic view of the relation of the Holy Spirit to the institutional church see George Hendry's *Gospel of the Incarnation.* Hendry's emphasis upon the Holy Spirit as the only true re-presentation of Christ is, I believe, the proper emphasis.

[6] See Wace and Bucheim's edition of *Luther's Primary Works,* Vol. XXII. p. 142; Vol. XXVII. p. 108.

[7] *Institutes* IV: I, 9.

[8] Ibid., IV: XIV, 1

[9] Lesslie Newbigin, *The Household of God: Lectures on the Nature of the Church* (New York: Friendship Press, 1954), p. 51; pp. 94-122.

[10] H. Wheeler Robinson, *The Christian Experience of the Holy Spirit* (New York: Harper and Brothers), p. 9.

[11] Clark Pinnock, "Opening the Church to the Charismatic Dimension," *Christianity Today* (June 12, 1981), p. 16.

[12] The enduring insight of Schweizer in this book, as far as this writer is concerned, is his conclusion that the structures of the Church must reflect both the freedom of the Spirit and the continuity of God's grace.

[13] Cited in *The Church is Charismatic,* p. 27.

[14]The author is indebted to Daniel Jenkins for the remark. It was made during a series of lectures on "The Church and the Radicalness of Christian Faith" given at Princeton Theological Seminary in the fall of 1981.

[15]Hollis Gause, "Society for Pentecostal Studies Newsletter," (Lee College, Cleveland, TN.), April, 1973.

[16]Robert McAfee Brown, *Frontiers for the Church Today* (New York: Oxford University Press, 1973), pp. 81-90.

Chapter 8

The Mission of the Holy Spirit

The Missionary Task

Christian missions is the fulfillment of God's redemptive purpose. "The enterprise known as worldwide missions," Robert Glover said, "is simply the carrying into effect of the divine purpose and project from the foundation of the world. Its accomplishment is the one sublime event toward which the whole creation moves forward, and which will constitute the consummation and crown of all God's dealings with the human race."[1]

The Bible is a missionary book from beginning to end. Scriptural authority for worldwide missions does not merely rest upon a group of proof texts, but upon the entire design and spirit of the Bible. Missions is the heart and soul of God. In contrast with all other sacred books, which are the story of man's search for God, the Bible is the story of God's search for man. God himself is the great Missionary. In Jesus Christ, God makes provision for the salvation of the whole world and sends His Son to redeem and reconcile the lost. The responsibility of those who have heard and received the "good news" is to tell others. Every Christian has a responsibility for the missionary task.

Yet, we know that a sense of duty and responsiblility alone is not sufficient motivation for the Church to bear witness to its Lord. The only sufficient witness to Jesus Christ is the Holy Spirit. Just as Jesus represented the

Father, the Holy Spirit now represents the Son. Jesus promised the Holy Spirit to His disciples so that they could effectively bear witness to Him. Some reference to the Holy Spirit is either made directly or implied in every one of the five statements of the Great Commission (Matthew 28:18-20; Mark 16:15:20; Luke 24:46-49; John 20:21, 22; Acts 1:8). Until the church received the Spirit at Pentecost, it was not really ready to be the Church. "Tarrying in Jerusalem" for the Holy Spirit was the necessary prerequisite for the Church "going into all the world and preaching the gospel." Christian missions and Pentecost were inseparably related. Pentecost was the essential preparation for missions. Missions was the logical and inevitable result of Pentecost.[2]

MOTIVATION FOR MISSION

The Christian mission could not really begin until the descent of the Holy Spirit at Pentecost, and Christian missions cannot effectively continue apart from the power and presence of the Spirit in the lives of those who witness to Jesus Christ. In his book entitled, *The Holy Spirit and Missions*, A. J. Gordon wrote: "Whenever in any period of the Church's history a little company has sprung up so surrendered to the Spirit and so filled with His presence as to furnish the pliant instruments of His will, then a new Pentecost has dawned in Christendom, and as a consequence the Great Commission has been republished; and following a fresh tarrying in Jerusalem for the enduement of power has been a fresh witnessing for Christ from Jerusalem to the uttermost parts of the earth."[3]

The Church does not actively witness to Jesus Christ until it has been moved and equipped by the Holy Spirit. Even the Apostolic church was relatively inactive until its members were moved by the Spirit into the streets of Jerusalem, to the regions of Judea and Samaria, and finally unto the ends of the earth. The church we read about in the Book of Acts did not become what it was until new energies were released at Pentecost. Jesus had accomplished His vocation in the power of the

Spirit. The church had to carry out its mission in the same power.

PENTECOST AND THE GREAT COMMISSION

The ministry of Jesus presupposed the Church for it was through the Church that God willed Christ's ministry to be continued. Conversely, the Church presupposes Christ for He is the reason for the Church's existence, the message which it proclaims. The Church of Jesus Christ exists for the purpose of witnessing. During His ministry Jesus gathered a nucleus of the Church together for the purpose of continuing His vocation after the ascension. It would be their responsibility to bear witness to what they had seen and heard (Acts 1:21). With the giving of the Great Commission, the Church received its official mandate from the Lord. Gospel witnessing was not to be one activity among many other activities of the Church. This was to be its essential activity, the law of the Church's life. There would be an organic relationship between Christ's mandate to witness and the life of the Church. The Church's witness would be an expression of its life; the church's life would depend upon its witness.

The Great Commission was given in connection with Pentecost. The commandment to go into all the world, preach Christ, and make disciples was entirely dependent upon the outpouring of the Holy Spirit. The Great Commission could only be carried out by a Pentecostal church, in Pentecostal power.[4] The church today is no less dependent upon the Holy Spirit. It must be baptized in Pentecostal power. There are many reasons why the Holy Spirit is necessary for missions.

First, it is not our witness alone, but it is the witness of the Holy Spirit through us, that convicts and convinces the world. Human instruments are important and necessary means through which God has willed to work His saving purpose, but it is ultimately the witness of the Spirit that accomplishes God's saving purpose. Is this not what Jesus meant when He said, "The Spirit of truth will bear witness to me; and you also are witnesses"? And, "Do not be anxious how you are to speak or what you are to say . . . for it is not you who speak, but the Spirit of your Father speaking through you" (See John 16:8; 15:26, 27; Matthew 10:19, 20.). With respect to evangelistic results, the record in Acts speaks for itself. No subsequent generation's record can compare with that period covered by the Acts of the Apostles. Why? Because the early Christians were more dynamic in their approach? Because their techniques were superior? Because they had learned the principles of church growth? Not really. It was because the Holy Spirit was at work, convicting and convincing those who heard the Word, of sin, righteousness, and judgment (John 16:8-11). Sinners do not come to God except they are drawn by the Holy Spirit.

Second, the church today needs the same courage and boldness to witness which the Holy Spirit gave Christians in Acts. Those already converted needed empowerment by the Spirit to witness. Before Pentecost, the apostolic band sequestered themselves, fearful of the Jews—pondering, no doubt, an uncertain future. Peter had quailed before the pointed finger of a servant girl and denied his Lord. What the early church needed most was courage and boldness. The pouring out of the Spirit by the resurrected Christ at Pentecost gave the church this power. After that, the record in Acts tells us what happened. Peter boldly charged the Sanhedrin with the murder of the Prince of life (Acts 2:23; 3:15; 4:8-10). When Peter and John were arraigned before Jewish rulers, Acts records that, "When they [the Jews] saw the boldness of Peter and John, and perceived that they were unlearned and ignorant men, they marvelled; and they took knowledge of them, that they had been with Jesus" (4:13). Their demeanor and speech, no doubt, bore witness to their courage and power. Stephen, the first Christian martyr, was arrested and subjected to false accusations and insults. Luke tells us that, "All that sat in the council, looking stedfastly on him, saw his face as it had been the face of an angel" (6:15). The record of what the Holy Spirit did in the lives of Christian believers in Acts is no less impressive than what He did in convicting and converting unbelievers.

Third, it is the Holy Spirit that gives the church direction and missionary motivation. Several instances are recorded in Acts where Christian workers were sent forth under the authority of the Holy Spirit. Philip was called from an evangelistic campaign in Samaria and sent by the Spirit to one lone Ethiopian in the desert (Acts 8:26, 29, 39). Human strategy would not dictate that an evangelist leave a successful evangelistic campaign where multitudes were hearing the gospel and signs were being manifested and go to the desert and minister to a confused African. But divine strategy was at work, preparing a witness for the Dark Continent which had as yet had no gospel witness.

The Holy Spirit broke through the prejudices of Peter and sent him to Caesarea, extending the gospel message to the Gentile world (chapter 10). In chapter thirteen of Acts, the Holy Spirit directed local church leaders at Antioch to "Separate Barnabas and Saul for the work whereunto he had called them." The Scripture records that they were "sent forth by the Holy Spirit" (13:4). What a beautiful picture of harmony and cooperation between the divine and human agencies in the call and appointment of Christian workers. Because the Holy Spirit had called them and sent them forth, He also empowered them to witness (13:9) and sustained them through trial and opposition (13:52). The gospel was then being taken beyond Jerusalem "unto the uttermost part of the earth" (1:8).

The Holy Spirit provided direction as well as impetus. When Paul and his party started again on a preaching tour into the province of Asia, they were restrained by the Holy Spirit from going into Asia a second time until the gospel had been preached in Europe. In a vision the "Man of Macedonia" guided Paul and his missionary party into a mission field where the gospel had not yet been preached (16:6-10). Glover reminds us that the Holy Spirit has exercised a similar form of restraint and constraint throughout the annals of missionary history. "Livingstone sought to go to China, but God suffered him not, but sent him to Africa. Carey's first thought was to go to the South Seas, but God guided him to

India. Judson planned to labor in India, but was driven to Burma by forces which in themselves were inimical, but which proved to be providential. That the Holy Spirit makes no mistakes is gloriously illustrated by the subsequent careers of these great missionary pioneers."[5]

Fourth, the church needs the administrative oversight of the Holy Spirit. The Holy Spirit is the Administrator-in-chief of the entire missionary movement. Organization, statesmanship, and strategy are important facets of the missionary enterprise, but without divine power and leadership they amount to very little. Paul reminded the elders of the church at Ephesus of the Holy Spirit's supreme authority: "Take heed therefore unto yourselves, and to all the flock, over the which the Holy Ghost hath made you overseers" (Acts 20:28).

In the early church there was no attempt to substitute human mechanics for divine dynamics. As a consequence, the church discovered that the Holy Spirit would even meet with and direct deliberative councils. Because of the recognized presence of the Holy Spirit in the deliberations of the Jerusalem council, the leaders of the council could say of their decisions, "It seemed good to the Holy Ghost and to us" (15:28). What a difference it would make in our decision making today if we were always conscious of and open to the leadership of the Spirit. How it would cut down on petty jealousies, bitter rivalries, and worldly wisdom.

Administering spiritual discipline and encouraging financial giving are two of the most difficult tasks of a church leader. But when the Holy Spirit administered the affairs of the church in Acts, He handled these difficult matters with divine ease. Because the Holy Spirit was the acknowledged Leader in the church, the sin of Ananias and Sapphira was in actuality an affront to the Holy Spirit. Peter did not charge the guilty couple with lying to him but to the Holy Spirit: "Why hath Satan filled thine heart to lie to the Holy Ghost?" and "How is it that ye have agreed together to tempt the Spirit of the Lord?" (5:3, 9). When the Holy Spirit's presence is manifest, genuine believers will be attracted while false professors will be restrained. The presence of the Spirit of God has a purifying effect in the local church. The two-fold effect of the Spirit's judgment of Ananias and Sapphira was that "believers were added to the Lord," while "none of the rest dared join them—but . . . held them in high honor" (5:13, 14; *RSV).*[6]

The Spirit's working in the early church was so evident that it inspired a new and unprecedented standard of giving. Without compulsion or intimidation the people voluntarily sold their possessions and brought the proceeds to the apostles for distribution (4:32, 34, 35). "There was not a needy person among them," the Scripture says, for they distributed to every man as they had need (vv. 34, 35). What a witness it would be today for the church to be similarly inspired by the Holy Spirit to care for its own poor and aged. It is in the context of their Spirit-inspired giving that Luke says, "With great power gave the apostles witness of the resurrection of the Lord Jesus: and great grace was upon them all" (v. 33). What we do with our possessions is one of the truest indicators of what the Holy Spirit has been able to effect in us.

THE MISSIONARY MEANING OF PENTECOST

It has been said that Jesus did not leave the Church with a philosophy but with a set of active verbs. This may explain why the finest expressions of appreciation for the role of the Holy Spirit in the life of the witnessing church have usually come from those most actively involved in missions. Those who are actively involved in the struggles and triumphs of the missionary enterprise seem to have a special appreciation for the Spirit's role in witnessing. Like weapons of war, the worth of the Spirit can be more appreciatively assessed on the field of action. Christ did not promise the Church His presence amidst their inactivity. He promises to be with the Church, in the person of the Holy Spirit, as they "Go" and "Tell" and "Make disciples." The work of the Holy Spirit is tied to action, to our action as witnesses. There is no promise of power where there is no witness, for the power exists for that purpose.

Many erroneous interpretations have arisen which

either distort or obscure the true meaning of Pentecost. Some are recent, but others can be traced in the Christian tradition for hundreds of years. Higher critics who attempt to determine the meaning of the biblical text by following the method of scientific investigation have found the event of Pentecost difficult to interpret. Working from a naturalistic, anti-supernaturalist bias, many have regarded the event as a piece of creative fiction propagated by the early church to explain its unknown origin and to legitimize the universal significance of its message.[7]

More conservative interpretations generally acknowledge the historicity of Pentecost, but they usually focus on the phenomenon of "speaking in tongues" and interpret this as a symbol of the universal diffusion of the gospel (Acts 2:1-13). While they admit the facticity of the event, they obscure its meaning by reducing it to a conscious Christian counterpart to the confusion of tongues at Babel (Genesis 11). Others understand Pentecost to represent covenant renewal because it was previously associated with the renewal of the covenant and the giving of the Law at Sinai in Jewish thought.[8] Elements of truth may be present in these associations, but none of them represent Luke's interpretation of Pentecost.

The most influential interpretation of Pentecost, however, was one which prevailed in Christendom for some 1,800 years—from the time of the church fathers, through the Middle Ages, continuing through the Reformation and post-Reformation period well into the nineteenth century. I am referring to that interpretation which understood the phenomenon of Acts 2 to mean that the purpose of Pentecost was to supernaturally endow the apostles and disciples of Christ with the ability to speak languages previously unknown to them for the purpose of missionary activity. As late as 1840, for example, the distinguished missionary, Alexander Duff, wrote concerning what was then the current view of Pentecost: "Take the gift of tongues:—wherein did it consist? Was it not this:—that into whatever city or region an apostle entered, he found himself instantly, without any previous study, and solely by supernatural communication, enabled to address the native inhabitants in their own vernacular dialect."[9]

Unlike that of the modern critic, this older view stressed the historical and supernatural character of the Pentecostal event. But like many modern interpretations, its stress fell upon the phenomenon of tongues speaking. The significance of Pentecost as empowerment for the missionary task of the church was little understood or appreciated apart from the belief that the gift of the Holy Spirit had enabled the apostles to speak foreign languages which they had not learned for the success of their missionary labors. The implications which were drawn from this interpretation were broadly inimical to the cause of the gospel.

This interpretation of Pentecost opposed its true intent because it raised that which was secondary to a place of primary importance. In this interpretation, the emphasis is upon "speaking in tongues" (a wrong emphasis) and on tongues as an enablement to speak languages one has not learned. It obscures the real intent of Pentecost which revealed the full extent to which the Holy Spirit is the determinative factor in the Church's missionary task. It confuses the symbols of the reality (that is, tongues, fire, wind, and so forth) with the reality itself (the Holy Spirit). What is meant to be seen in the event of Pentecost is the vital place of the Holy Spirit in making Christ real and present through the witness of the Church. Pentecost shows us how the Church was reconstituted into a prophetic body by the Holy Spirit so that it might effectively bear witness to Jesus Christ.

This interpretation also misrepresented the meaning of the Pentecostal event by denying its power as an ongoing reality in the church. Those who held to this view were generally dispensationalist in outlook. That is, they viewed what happened at Pentecost as something meant only for the apostles and the apostolic period. There was no expectation that the reality of Pentecost should continue. The result, of course, was that this interpretation discouraged any real openness to the power of the Spirit. One is not likely to be receptive to that which they have been conditioned against. The demise of this interpretation, however, was inevitable because it had both the weight of Scripture and history against it. All that supported it was a theological bias that was fated to be exposed.[10]

The only sound interpretation of Pentecost is Jesus' interpretation, as recorded in Acts 1:8—"But you will receive power when the Holy Spirit comes on you; and you will be my witnesses in Jerusalem, and in all Judea and Samaria, and to the ends of the earth" (NIV). Jesus' announcement interprets the event; the event does not define itself. Jesus' interpretation of Pentecost lets us know that glossolalia, or speaking in tongues, was not the primary significance of Pentecost. Speaking in tongues, as the 120 did in Acts 2, is more than ecstatic speech or a supernatural ability to speak languages that one has never learned. The supernatural phenomenon of "speaking in other tongues as the Spirit gives the utterance" points to the fact that the Spirit is bestowed primarily for the purpose of gospel transmission. He is the necessary power through which the gospel of Christ is transmitted to the world through the church. The repeatable reality in Pentecost is the power to bear witness and praise to Jesus Christ. Speaking in tongues is the outward physical evidence of this power.[11]

Spirit and speaking belong together. Spirit and Word cannot be separated. The Church came into being in its New Testament form as a speaking, proclaiming, praising body. It was not a parochial or privitized message. The church addressed all men from all nations with her message (Acts 2:5-11).[12] Luke gives prominence to the "speaking with other tongues" because of its association with the speaking, witnessing, and praising God that occurred.

This is consistent with the fact that the first event recorded after the outpouring of the Holy Spirit is Peter's sermon (that is, gospel proclamation). One also notes Paul's admonition that, above all, one should desire to prophesy. Paul did not discourage devotional tongues (that is, uninterpreted tongues), when exercised in an orderly fashion, but he taught that tongues could only benefit the unbeliever when they became intelligible through interpretation. The church needs both to speak the Word and to have the Word spoken to it. It is the church's responsibility to communicate that Word which it has received from God.

It is biblically sound to say that "speaking in other tongues is the initial [and, it ought to be added, 'continuing'] evidence of Spirit-baptism" for Word and Spirit cannot be separated. What has oftentimes been regarded as a sectarian distinctive is, in fact, one of the most prominent teachings of the New Testament. The fullness of the Spirit is always evidenced by speaking, witnessing, and praising God (Acts 2:11).

Pentecost brought the church an experience of intensified power, but it also brought the church an awareness of the need to extend that power to the whole world. At Pentecost, the Holy Spirit began to make the life of the New Age operative in the church. Powers that alienated and divided were overcome by the Holy Spirit. Walls of partition which divided Jew and Gentile, male and female, Greek and barbarian, were broken down. The post-Pentecost church gave witness by precept and example to a gospel that frees and liberates. Acts is the story of an unbound gospel set free from its Jewish origins to penetrate the whole world. Pentecostal penetration into virtually every culture and strata of society in the twentieth century is further evidence that gospel witness is most effective when the church is empowered for mission by the Holy Spirit. History proves the error of those who teach that Pentecost was only meant for the apostolic era. As long as there is a need for gospel proclamation and witness, there will be a need for Pentecostal power such as was given in Acts 2.

Adolph Harnack once noted that, "history is the best way to overcome history." History itself has debunked the theory that the meaning and power of Pentecost were temporary. The view that the experience of Pentecost was only meant for the apostles and their immediate successors, that its miraculous power ceased at the close of the apostolic era, has fallen victim to historical reality.[13]

The Apostle Peter was the first to emphasize that Pentecostal empowerment was for "all flesh," as Joel had prophesied (Acts 2:16; Joel 2:28-32). There is no indication in Scripture that empowerment for witness was ever meant to be limited to one generation or time span. The outpouring of the Holy Spirit in subsequent periods of Church history, especially our own, is evidence that this is not the case.

When the Pentecostal revival broke out in Kansas, Texas, California, North Carolina, and Tennessee at the beginning of this century, the movement itself became a witness to the significance of Pentecost. Evangelism and missions virtually became synonymous with the Pentecostal experience. When the movement showed evidence of turning inward, there was a fresh outpouring of the Spirit upon once nominal church groups. Since the late '50s, the Spirit has been experienced in extraordinary ways in practically every historic denomination. Anglicans, Catholics, Lutherans, Presbyterians, Baptists, Methodists, Mennonites, Quakers, Salvation Army, and other groups too numerous to mention have experienced the dynamic moving of the Holy Spirit. The penetration of the Holy Spirit has known no boundaries. As He did in the early church, the Holy Spirit has hurdled every socioeconomic, racial, and national barrier.

History confirms what Scripture teaches. Wherever the Holy Spirit is allowed to fully work, he transforms the church into a witnessing and worshipping body.[14] People speak freely today of theological renewal, liturgical renewal, structural renewal, pastoral renewal, and the renewal of the laity. The important fact of Pentecost is that whenever and wherever the Holy Spirit is allowed to freely operate, the church will be renewed in all dimensions of its life so that it can truly be the witnessing and worshiping body that Christ intended it to be. It was that way in the apostolic church; it can be that way today.

THE RECONSTITUTION OF THE CHURCH

One of Luke's emphases in Acts 2 is that the outpouring of the Holy Spirit represented the fulfillment of a long-awaited promise. This promise extended back to the promise of Joel that in the last days the Spirit of God would be poured out on "all flesh" (Joel 2:28). The promise was taken up by John the Baptist and continued by Jesus who promised His disciples that they would receive power to witness when the Spirit came upon them (Matthew 3:11; Acts 1:8). Pentecost is presented by Luke as the fulfillment of a promise that the mission of the church would be an essential part of God's salvation plan.[15] This plan would be fulfilled in the power of the Spirit.

Jesus' promise of the Holy Spirit in Acts 1:8, and its fulfillment in Acts 2, is particularly important because it is programmatic for the whole Book of Acts. The story of missionary outreach that runs throughout the Book of Acts is directly related to what happened at Pentecost. The Holy Spirit so empowered the church for witness that the gospel was literally taken to the farthest parts of the world before their generation had passed. In the minds of the gospel writers the Church's mission was closely related to the end of the age. In response to His disciple's question concerning the sign of His second coming and the end of the world, Jesus responded that, "this gospel shall be preached in all the world for a witness to all nations; and then shall the end come" (Matthew 24:3, 14). The mission and the end (that is, the eschaton) were vitally linked. The church existed for a witnessing function. But it could not fulfill its intended function as a witnessing community until it had been reconstituted by the Holy Spirit. The new wine of the Spirit needed new institutional wineskins. Until Pentecost, the institutions through which the church ministered were constituted relative to Judaism. At Pentecost, the church was reconstituted relative to the ministry of the Spirit.

Before Pentecost, the Temple was the central place of worship, the priest the central office-bearer, the altar the central cultic object, and the sacrifice the central cultic act. In Judaism, the object of prophecy lay ahead. The prophet could speak of God's action in the present, but the expectation of the Messiah pointed to the future.[16]

Christ's coming changed all that. It was now the work of the Holy Spirit to reconstitute the Church in accordance with the new situation. Jesus' conversation with the woman of Samaria revealed that the period for Temple worship had come to an end. "The hour cometh," Jesus said, "when ye shall neither in this mountain, nor yet at Jerusalem, worship the Father . . . the hour cometh, and now is, when the true worshippers shall worship the Father in spirit and in truth: for the Father seeketh such to worship him. God is a Spirit: and they that worship him must worship him in spirit and in truth" (John 4:21, 23, 24). Jewish worship centered in the Temple. True worship of God could now take place anywhere worship was offered in spirit and truth.

In Judaism, the sacerdotal duties of the priest were all-important. But the eternal sacrifice on the altar of the cross abrogated forever any need for types and shadows that anticipated Christ. After Calvary the witness was no longer forward looking—to One that was to come; the witness was now to One who had already come whose completed work would constitute the focus of New Testament revelation. Prophecy was now primarily a matter of gospel proclamation. The Supper was a remembrance of Christ's finished work (1 Corinthians 11:24-26). Those gifted for ministry by the Holy Spirit would have as their task to bear witness to Jesus Christ, the new reality (Ephesians 4:11,12). In this New Age of the Spirit one did not have to have a special office to prophesy. Joel foretold that the Holy Spirit would come on "all flesh," that even the "sons and daughters would prophesy" (Joel 2:28). Luke tells us that at Pentecost they were "all" filled with the Holy Ghost and "began to speak" (Acts 2:4).

At Pentecost, a dissemination of the prophetic function occurred which not only fulfilled the prophecy of Joel but the desire of Moses who said that he "would that all the Lord's people were prophets" (Numbers 11:29; RSV). Isaiah's expectation was that the pouring out of the Lord's Spirit would be followed by a confession of the Lord's name (Isaiah 44:5). Pentecost signaled the reconstitution of the church for witness by "all" who are filled with the Spirit.

"Acts is governed by one dominant, overriding and all-controlling motif," Harry Boer wrote a generation ago:

> This motif is the expansion of the faith through missionary witness in the power of the Spirit. . . .
> One hardly knows where in Acts to look for a distinction between Church and missions. Restlessly the Spirit drives the Church to witness, and continually churches rise out of the witness. The Church is a missionary Church. She is not missionary Church in the sense that she is 'very much interested' in missions, or that she 'does a great deal' for missions. In Acts missions is not a hobby of an 'evangelical section' of the Church. The Church as a whole is missionary in all her relationships . . . the missionary witness of Acts is inseparable from the Church; it is equally inseparable from the Spirit.[17]

When believers are filled with the Spirit, the Great Commission becomes the law of their life. Jesus indicated what believers would be, as well as do, when they are filled with the Spirit: "You will be my witnesses" (Acts 1:8, *NIV*).

Until the Church received the Holy Spirit it was not equipped to be the Church, to carry out its mission. After Pentecost it could not but carry out its mission. The Book of Acts shows us the intensity of the Spirit's influence, but it also shows us the extent of the church's witness. For the early church was not content until it had taken the gospel unto the "uttermost parts of the earth." When Christians today receive the Holy Spirit as the 120 did on the Day of Pentecost, they too are empowered for mission. The same Spirit that empowered Jesus for His ministry empowers those who continue His ministry in the world.

WITNESSING TO THE WHOLE JESUS

Witness terminology in the New Testament is primarily concentrated in two sections: Luke-Acts and John. In John, the witness emphasis is on Jesus' person—His identity and authorization (1:14, 34; 5:36; 16:7-11). In Luke-Acts, the emphasis falls more on the witness to Jesus' life and ministry—on the things which Jesus' followers had seen and heard with their own eyes (Luke 1:1-4; 24:46-48; Acts 1:21).

Luke's stress in Acts is on the Church's mission and the importance of the Holy Spirit for the actualization of that mission. His intent is to emphasize the witness effect of the Holy Spirit, not the ethical effects of the Spirit. The gift of the Spirit at Pentecost is seen by Luke as the equipping of the Church for mission by giving it boldness and power to proclaim the gospel.[18] What Luke stresses about the Holy Spirit was altogether right and necessary. But as I. Howard Marshall notes, "An account of the Spirit's activity which is based solely on the Pentecost story is one-sided and inadequate; the Pentecost story is concerned solely with mission, and stresses the importance of this aspect of the Spirit's work. In one sense, therefore, the Church cannot be content merely with a repetition of 'Pentecost.' It needs an experience involving other dimensions of the Spirit's activity."[19] For the Church to witness truly and effectively to the whole Jesus it must not neglect the Spirit's ethical work in the believer.

The witness of the church has never been right nor effective when separated from the Holy Spirit's sanctifying grace. "The Christ-filled life is the surest evidence and witness to the Spirit-filled life," Hollis Gause writes.[20] And, of course, the reverse is also true. Pentecost is empowerment for Christlike living.

The witness to Jesus Christ which the Holy Spirit inspires and empowers is the witness of one's life as well as one's lips. There can be no separation between the preaching of the Kingdom and the ethical demands of the Kingdom itself. "The preaching of the Kingdom makes certain ethical demands," Gause explains:

In preparation for the coming of the King and the manifestation of the Kingdom, paths must be cleared and straightened. This was enforced by the ethical demands made by John the Baptist in his proclamation. What he required in his preaching was inseparable from the Kingdom which he announced . . . evidence of repentance in terms of restitution, changed lives, and a repudiation of the old life.

The ministry of Jesus combined even more specifically the spiritual and ethical demands of the Kingdom which He proclaimed. We need no greater evidence for this claim than the Sermon on the Mount (Matthew 5-7). It is made warp and woof of the Kingdom and its proclamation.

The Holy Spirit, as the gift of God for the last days, enforces the same union of spiritual and moral duty with the formation of the Kingdom. If the Holy Spirit—the eschatological gift to the kingdom of God—is also present, we ought therefore to live in existential crisis: to live as those who stand in the presence of the coming glorious and holy King.[21]

Those who are called to witness are also called to righteousness and holy living.[22] A Spirit-controlled witness cannot be separated from a Spirit-controlled walk. The Spirit's witness to Christ is one in which deed cannot be separated from word, nor precept from example. Jesus' witness to the Father was complete and believable because there was never any discrepancy between what Jesus taught and what Jesus exemplified. The same, of course, must be true for those who witness to Christ today. The closer our walk is connected with our witness, the more of Jesus we witness to and the more believable our testimony. The Christ who has been revealed to us must be formed in us by the Holy Spirit.

There is an aspect of witnessing to the whole Jesus which is sorely missing in many testimonies; namely, that testimony to Christ which can be seen and felt through our identification with the needs of the poor and oppressed. There is a tendency today to polarize "activists" and "evangelicals," to separate those who would save souls from those who would feed the hungry, clothe the naked, and liberate the oppressed. Such labels are misleading and distort the gospel message. One would advocate a half-Jesus of evangelism without social action, the other a half-Jesus of activism without evangelism.[23] When isolated, both ultimately fail because neither focuses clearly on the true object of the church's witness, Jesus Christ. Jesus himself set the parameters of the Church's vision and witness when He said, "Ye shall be witnesses unto me" (Acts 1:8). When Jesus shapes our witness, there cannot be one without the other. The Word of God which we preach must become incarnate in our flesh if we are to continue the ministry of Christ in the world through the Spirit. The Church cannot bear witness to Jesus in a way that is faithful to Scripture without becoming involved in human need and suffering.

Interestingly enough, it is Luke the missionary evangelist who sets forth Jesus' programmatic action as one which has social as well as personal redemptive significance. When Jesus returned to Nazareth after His period of temptation in the wilderness, Luke records Jesus' announcement of the purpose of His Spirit-anointed ministry:

> The Spirit of the Lord is upon me, because he has anointed me to preach good news to the poor. He has sent me to proclaim release to the captives and recovering of sight to the blind, to set at liberty those who are oppressed, to proclaim the acceptable year of the Lord (Luke 4:18, 19; RSV; see Isaiah 61:1, 2).

What Jesus read to the Jews in the Synagogue that day from Isaiah had for its setting the Old Testament teaching regarding the Jubilee and Sabbath Year. During this time the poor were released from debt, the oppressed were set free, and all were reminded that the Lord owns the land and gives it to His people for stewardship (Leviticus chapter 25 and Deuteronomy chapter 15). There was no distinction in the Mosaic Law between religious and social duty. One could not rightly be considered religious apart from the fulfillment of

social responsibility. The prophets were always critical
of cleavages between true religion and social justice. In
Isaiah 58, a companion text to Isaiah 61 from which
Jesus read in the Synagogue, the prophet sternly rebuked
the people for maintaining cultic observances that were
devoid of social compassion:

> Is not this the fast that I choose:
>   to loose the bonds of wickedness,
>   to undo the thongs of the yoke,
>   to let the oppressed go free,
>   and to break every yoke?

> Is it not to share your bread with the hungry,
> and bring the homeless poor into your house;
> when you see the naked, to cover him, and not
>   to hide yourself from your own flesh?

(Isaiah 58:6, 7; *RSV*).

When Jesus applied the fulfillment of Isaiah 61 to His
messianic mission, He was presenting Himself as the
liberating reality of the New Age. Jesus and His messianic
ministry inaugurated the present/future eschatological
salvation of God.[24] As Daniel Migliore puts it, His ministry would be "ultimately decisive, definitive, archetypal
for our relationship with God, with other persons, and
with society."[25] Jesus' self-understanding of His mission
as one of liberation gives meaning and definition to our
own as the people of God.

The key term used by Jesus in His reading from
Isaiah 61, with its setting in the jubilee or sabbath year
legislation, was the term release. Jubilee year legislation
provided relief for the poor and the oppressed, held in
bondage to poverty and debt, but it could not offer
deliverance from the oppression of sin and guilt. For
this redemptive mission, the Spirit of God anointed
Jesus of Nazareth who proclaimed the good news of the
gospel to the poor and released those who were captive
to sin. Jesus' message and ministry was one of redemptive release.

The debt forgiveness which Jesus offered was the
divine act of forgiving sin. Jesus liberated from sin, the
curse of the Law, and the powers of this world. "For

freedom Christ has set us free," Paul wrote to the Galatians (5:1). But Christ not only offered release from the penalty of sin, He offered release from the power and consequences of sin which bind us and make us to be filled with dis-"ease." Jesus offered wholeness. The deliverance and release which Jesus offered were signs that the New Age had arrived. To the question of the imprisoned John who asked if Jesus was the Christ, or if he should look for another, Jesus sent word: "The blind receive their sight, and the lame walk, the lepers are cleansed, and the deaf hear, the dead are raised up, and the poor have the gospel preached to them" (Matthew 11:5).

Jesus demonstrated a special concern for outcasts and those discriminated against by society—lepers, Samaritans, women, the poor. His gospel was so elevating and transforming that Paul could write after Jesus what would have been utterly inconceivable to a Jew one generation earlier, that "there is neither Jew nor Greek, there is neither slave nor free, there is neither male nor female; for you are all one in Christ Jesus" (Galatians 3:28; RSV). Unlike those who used the Law to bind, Jesus challenged every interpretation of the Law that made it an instrument of human bondage.

In word and deed, Jesus revealed that God calls men beyond the idols of this world—nation, race, wealth, power, and so forth. He called men from their bondage to materialism and power and set them free for service. He freed them not only from spiritual death but from the terror of death itself. Jesus revealed that God stands against all forms of oppression, regardless of their source. Those who would justify any form of oppression in the name of God do not know the God who is revealed in Jesus Christ.

In Jesus Christ, God redemptively releases the poor and the oppressed. But the redeemed are freed for a purpose. They are not like F. Scott Fitzgerald who said he was like a little boy alone in a big house, who could do anything he wanted to do, but suddenly discovered that there was nothing he wanted to do. Christians have been converted from their sins, but they have been converted for their neighbor. Just as Jesus was a Man-for-others, He frees us so that we may be a "Christ to our neighbor." The evangelical paradox of the gospel, Martin Luther said, is that a Christian is free, subject to none, yet the dutiful servant of all. The gospel frees us that the Holy Spirit might equip us for self-giving action.

The story is told of the little girl who kept calling her father to her room during a violent thunderstorm. After several visits, the father tried to comfort his young daughter by telling her that God was there and would take care of her. "Yes, Daddy, I know God is here," the little girl replied, "but right now I need somebody with skin on." The world would see Jesus, but they want to see a Jesus with skin on. They want to see Jesus enfleshed in believers. God wills that the love of God be experienced in the world through the senses, in the social order, by those for whom the love of God has been manifested in Jesus Christ.

Christians ought not to expect intimacy with Christ apart from a commitment to Christ's concern for others. We worship God directly through the Holy Spirit, but we serve God through our neighbor. What you do to your neighbor in need you do to the Lord Christ himself. "Inasmuch as ye have done it unto one of the least of these my brethren," Jesus said, "ye have done it unto me" (Matthew 25:40).

If we witness to the whole Jesus, we will witness to the Jesus who met the needs of the whole person. And if that witness is enfleshed in us, we ourselves will become part of God's answer. It is not enough for the church to function as a referral agency, turning people over to God without the benefit of their own Spirit-inspired concern.

Charles Beach, a well-known Christian layman in the Church of God, tells of a time when he was witnessing to an unsaved person about accepting Christ. The person to whom he was witnessing was having financial difficulties, and the family did not even have food in the house. My friend felt inspired to tell this person that he believed God would supply his material needs if he would first make a commitment to Jesus Christ as Savior and Lord. To his surprise, the person yielded to the conviction of the Holy Spirit and accepted Christ. Afterwards, they prayed about the physical needs of the family. He testifies that during the prayer it was as though the Lord spoke to him and said, "You are the answer to this prayer. Go and buy this family some groceries."

Social concern was never meant to be something tacked on to the gospel for good measure, to round it all out. Christian concern for human need and suffering is never a matter of adding something on; it is part of the gospel itself. Genuine concern and self-giving action toward others are the surest proofs we have of the gospel's power to penetrate and transform human life. Where faith is active in love, we know that the gospel is truly being communicated. Our love for Christ is not gauged by feelings as much as by actions. The concern and action we show for those in need is not a matter of choice for the Christian; it is the essence of being Christian.

Christianity is a catholic faith in that it is a faith for the entire human family, and it is a faith for the whole person. Every dimension of a person's life can be ministered to through the power of the Holy Spirit. Ours is a world of fragmented and unfinished people who need to be made whole. Jesus Christ is both the model and the means for wholeness. The Church's witness to the whole Jesus is the only hope which the human family has for finding that wholeness for which it was created.

A word of caution is in order. It is easy to admit to what we have said, to talk much about the power of the Spirit to transform human life and renew the created order. But many are quick to assign all such action to the future, to the coming eschaton when all life will be made new through a transformation of cosmic proportions. It is true that the final act of transformation must be God's, not our own. But we do violence to the instruction of Scripture and to the reality of the New Age, which Christ has already inaugurated, when we assign to the future what God has called us to participate in now. In Jesus Christ the inbreaking of the kingdom of God has already occurred. Through the power of the Holy Spirit, we participate now in the life made available through Christ. The church must not be like the gentleman at the train depot who was so caught up in the train schedules that he missed his train. The final victory of Christ has yet to be consummated, but the decisive victory has already been accomplished. The significance of that victory must not be lost in obscurity by eschatological futurism. God calls on us now to participate with Him, through the Spirit, in making all things new.

A degree of frustration and disappointment will always accompany our efforts to reclaim this world for Christ. But the sheer massiveness and complexity of human problems must not be allowed to overwhelm us so that we are paralyzed into inaction. Our labors always seem small and insignificant when viewed in light of the total task. But it is well to remember that we do not bear the burden of bringing the process to completion ourselves. The fulfillment of history can only come from beyond history. God can be trusted to consummate what He has chosen to begin through us. In the power of the Spirit, God calls upon us to live faithfully and productively in the interim between the "already" and the "not yet."

Life in the "already" dimension of the Spirit redeems us from paralysis and withdrawal from human need and suffering. The Holy Spirit will not allow us to fold our hands and close our eyes to human need. If we are walking in the Spirit, we will be the extended arms and hands of Jesus Christ. The "not yet" dimension, on the other hand, saves us from utopian thinking. We know that the consummation of God's kingdom will not come through growth in history. Christ must consummate and finalize that which has already begun. For that reason, the Holy Spirit within us will not cease to groan and long for the day of final redemption.

In the tension of the interim in which we live, the church is called to be the Church. When the church is empowered by the Holy Spirit it does not have to be linked with special interest groups or motivated by alien ideologies. Its action will be self-generated. The only terms under which the world can be truly liberated are Christ's terms. The only liberation movement the church needs to espouse is the one which already exists in Christ. Our responsibility is to express the liberation we already know in Jesus Christ. We have been "called out" for the purpose of re-presenting our Lord, claiming and refashioning as much as we can of that which is His by right.

FOOTNOTES

[1]Robert Hall Glover, *The Bible Basis of Missions*, (Los Angeles, California: The Bible House of Los Angeles, 1956), p. 14. Glover's treatment of missions, particularly the role of the Holy Spirit in missions, is one of the finest that I have read. This old classic is worthy of every Christian's attention.

[2]Ibid., p. 57.

[3]Ibid., p. 62.

[4]Ibid., p. 61.

[5]Ibid., p. 68.

[6]Ibid., p. 66.

[7]Eduard Ziller, Otto Pfleiderer, Johannes Weiss, Hans Hinrich Wendt, K. L. Schmidt, and Adolf Harnack were representative of the more extreme type of critical thinking about Pentecost. Many of these critics were in the tradition of F. C. Baur and the Tubingen School of higher criticism.

[8]For a scholarly analysis of various interpretations of Pentecost and a sound interpretation of his own, see I. Howard Marshall, "The Significance of Pentecost," *Scottish Journal of Theology*, vol. XXX, 1977, pp. 347-369.

[9]Alexander Duff, *India and India Missions* (Edinburgh, 1840), p. 378.

[10]A good modern example of this dispensational bias is Merrill F. Unger's *New Testament Teaching on Tongues*. The exegetical weaknesses in this work are obvious to any careful reader who does not read the book with Unger's theological bias.

[11]This is not meant to imply that speaking in tongues, as the Holy Spirit gives the utterance, is itself unimportant. What is most important, however, is the reality of Jesus Christ to whom the tongues give witness and praise.

[12]The universal mission of the Christian Church is graphically revealed through the event of Pentecost. The inseparable connection between the Great Commission and Pentecost is revealed through the events which transpired.

[13]Benjamin B. Warfield's *Miracles: Yesterday and Today* is a good

example of such a view. The historical reality of Pentecostalism and the charismatic movement is proof enough that this view is erroneous.

[14]Witnessing and worshiping have been the two essential ingredients in the success of Pentecostal churches, just as they were in the apostolic church.

[15]Marshall, p. 367.

[16]For an excellent treatment of the manner in which the Holy Spirit reconstituted the Church in accordance with its new situation, see a book by Henry Boer entitled, *Pentecost and Missions* (Grand Rapids, Michigan: Eerdmans, 1961).

[17]Ibid., pp. 153, 154.

[18]Marshall, p. 368.

[19]Ibid.

[20]Hollis Gause, "Society for Pentecostal Studies Newsletter," (Lee College, Cleveland, TN.), April, 1973.

[21]Hollis Gause, *Living in the Spirit* (Cleveland, TN.: Pathway Press, 1980), p. 97.

[22]Ibid., 95, 96. The Pentecostal ought never to emphasize the gifts of the Spirit at the expense of the fruit of the Spirit or vice versa. The truth of the matter is not an either/or but a both/and. For a beautifully balanced perspective see Charles W. Conn's *A Balanced Church*.

[23]Leander E. Keck, "Listening to and Listening For," *Interpretation* XXVII (April, 1973), pp. 193ff. Keck's article illustrates the danger in approaching biblical texts such as Acts 1:8 with an ideological mind-set.

[24]Robert Bryan Sloan, *The Favorable Year of the Lord: A Study of Jubilary Theology in the Gospel of Luke* (Austin, Texas: Schola Press, 1977), p. 166.

[25]Daniel L. Migliore, *Called to Freedom: Liberation Theology and the Future of Christian Doctrine* (Philadelphia: Westminster Press, 1980), p. 43.

Chapter 9

The Holy Spirit and Hope

Two Dimensions of Hope: The Future and The Present

Hope is an essential need of man. It is also one of the most prominent teachings of Scripture. Hope is not attached to the end of theology or to the periphery of theology but to the heart of the New Testament. Faith is the evidence of things "hoped for" (Hebrews 11:1). It is not just future promise but promise that has already begun to be fulfilled. The heathen, for Paul, are "those who have no hope" while Christians are those who "have been saved in hope" (see 1 Thessalonians 4:13; Romans 8:24). There is the promise of a future that has not yet arrived, but there is also the reality of the future that has already invaded the present. The message of the Incarnation and the Cross is that God is "for us," that through the Holy Spirit He indwells us now. The message of the Resurrection is that God is "ahead of us," that the fullness of God's purpose for our lives is yet to come. He already is but yet He is more to come.

Hopelessness and trust in false forms of hope are the twin tragedies of our time. No amount of money, health, friends, or learning can ever satisfy man's craving for something more than he presently possesses. And no amount of destitution or deprivation can destroy a person who has not lost hope. In his little classic, *Man's Search for Meaning*, Victor Frankl wrote: "Any attempt to restore man's inner strength in the camp [at Auschwitz] had first to succeed in showing him some future goal . . . woe to him who saw no more sense in his life, no aim, no purpose, and therefore no point in carrying on. He was soon lost."

Christianity does not promise an answer to all our questions about the present or the future. But it does give us the answer to the ultimate question: "If a man dies, will he live again?" This question is resolved by Christ's resurrection. Christian hope is not based on wishful thinking or Polly Annaish optimism that all is going to be sweetness and light. It is grounded in a historical reality. The New Testament assures us that ". . . according to His abundant mercy [God] has begotten us to a living hope through the resurrection of Jesus Christ from the dead" (1 Peter 1:3; *NKJ*).

Billy Graham relates the story of a meeting he had some years ago with Konrad Adenauer before he retired as the chancellor of West Germany. "When I walked in," Graham says, "I expected to meet a tall, stiff, formal man who might even be embarrassed if I brought up the subject of religion. After the greeting, the chancellor suddenly turned to me and said, 'Mr. Graham, what is the most important thing in the world?' Before I could answer, he answered his own question. He said, 'The resurrection of Jesus Christ. If Jesus Christ is alive, then there is hope for the world. If Jesus Christ is in the grave, then I don't see the slightest glimmer of hope on the horizon.' Then he amazed me by saying that the resurrection of Jesus Christ was one of the best-attested facts of history."

Chancellor Adenauer was right. The Christian hope is solidly grounded in the fact of Jesus' resurrection from the dead. But there is also another reason why the Christian lives with hope. According to the New Testament, hope is instilled in us by the Holy Spirit who has been poured into our hearts and bears witness within us that we are sons of God and fellow heirs with Christ (Romans 8:14-17). It is this grace-experience that enables us to "hope against hope" as others have whom Scripture commends. Hope goes beyond that which is tangible and can be objectively verified. Hope arises out of a deep preconceptual experience of God who communicates His love and concern for us through acts of grace. Hope is grace. It is God's presence in us now that assures us that our future in Him will be secure. Christian hope is grounded in God's historical action, but it results from the Spirit's indwelling presence. Both are essential to our understanding of Christian eschatology.

THE BACKGROUND OF JEWISH ESCHATOLOGY

The term eschatology comes from the Greek word *eschaton* which means "the last thing." The Hebrews were the first to recognize that history has a purposeful end, that all things are moving toward an end which God has foreordained.[1] Because of God's purposeful activity in their own history the Hebrews believed in a purposeful creation and movement of historical events. Early Jewish eschatology lacked clear definition. The future was unclear because the purpose of creation and the meaning of the historical process had not been fully revealed. But there was hope for the future because of God's meaningful activity in the past. God was sovereign, and His activity in the history of the covenant people could only portend hope for the future. At the time of the Exile the major prophets prophesied a future age when a messiah would come, the dead would be raised, and the Spirit would revivify the nation. The "present age" with its evil and suffering would be consummated and transformed into a time of peace and blessing. In the end-time a restoration would occur. The primeval conditions which existed before the Fall would be restored. A renewal of the old creation would result in something new, a "new creation" for a New Age.

Late Jewish eschatology centered in the messianic hope. Apocalyptic writers expected a time when God's rule would be established on earth under the Messiah. The resurrection of the dead was envisioned, and the Spirit of God was expected to renew the righteous. Judgment upon sin and evil would follow. God's sovereign will would prevail in the Age to Come. The unrighteous would suffer righteous retribution; the righteous would enjoy God's righteous reign.

The so-called "apocalyptic" literature of the Old Testament (for example, parts of Daniel, Ezekiel, Zechariah, and other books) expressed Israel's eschatological hopes. But apocalyptic hopes were shrouded in symbolism and mystery. They were not presented in systematic or easy-to-understand thought forms. The message of the apocalyptic literature could not be understood apart from its future fulfillment. Actual events and their order of occurrence could not be understood apart from their unfolding in history. The events themselves would provide the interpretive key for understanding the apocalyptic mysteries.

New Testament scholars generally agree that Jewish eschatology was one of the interpretive keys through which New Testament writers understood God's saving action in Jesus Christ. Eschatology was the key in understanding Jesus Christ and Jesus Christ was the key to understanding eschatology. Ernst Käsemann, a prominent New Testament scholar, goes so far as to call apocalyptic "The Mother of all Christian theology."[2] Käsemann may have overstated the case, but the fact that Jewish eschatology plays a prominent role in New Testament interpretation is undeniable. It is particularly true for Paul whose writings deal specifically with the meaning of his Jewish past in light of the resurrected Christ.

INTERPRETING HISTORY IN LIGHT OF JESUS CHRIST

Coming out of a background in rabbinic Judaism, Paul knew Jewish hopes and expectations. He also knew that Jesus Christ was the new fact in light of which all else had to be interpreted. The resurrection of Jesus from the dead had literally given history a new meaning. Jesus' resurrection and the presence of the Spirit could mean only one thing for Paul. The expected Age to Come was now present in the power of the Spirit. Not in its final cosmic dimensions, for the *parousia* (that is, the return of Christ in glory at the end of the age) still lay in the future, but the glory and power of the Age to Come had already been inaugurated in Jesus Christ and the coming of the Spirit. The New Age was already being tasted and experienced by believers through the Holy Spirit.

Until His resurrection, Jesus lived and died under the scrutiny of history. Even His closest followers had their doubts about Him. His enemies openly questioned His claims. They mocked Him and made cruel accusations of blasphemy against the claim of His divinity. Jesus' resurrection and the special outpouring of the Spirit at Pentecost changed that for those who experienced these realities. Resurrection faith now sat in judgment on all prior conceptions of history. Jewish eschatology, for Christian believers, would now be understood in light of these historical events.

The empty tomb and the experience of the life-giving Spirit combined to produce in Jesus' disciples the certainty of faith. This faith sustained them and provided the necessary impetus for their commission. The reception of the Holy Spirit was a necessary complement to the empty tomb. Peter's argument on the Day of Pentecost for the resurrection and ascension of Christ was an argument from the Spirit's witness. "This same Jesus God raised up," Peter said, "of which we all are witnesses; therefore, since he has been lifted up to the right hand of God and has received the promise of the Holy Spirit from the Father, he has poured out this which you both see and hear" (Acts 2:32, 33). The apostle attached the highest evidential value to the witness of the Holy Spirit. "Peter could have shown them an empty tomb," Hollis Gause points out:

> But an empty tomb does not prove the resurrection of the former occupant of the tomb. He could call eyewitnesses that had seen the resurrected Jesus, but he could not on this day show them Jesus in the flesh. The primary proof, then, of Christ's presence with the father is the outpouring of that Spirit whom the Father had promised . . . A personal Pentecost is our highest evidence of Christ's resurrection. This evidence rises above the evi-

dence of sight and argumentation. It is well and good to be able to point to the empty tomb, to show the physical evidence of resurrection, and to list all of the polemic arguments for resurrection; but the only saving evidence of the resurrection of Christ is the testimony of the Holy Spirit.[3]

After His resurrection, Jesus was openly acknowledged as the divine Son of God. He was the Lord of the Church by whom all other things would now be valued and judged. For Jesus' followers, He was the center of truth and value. Things now had value only in relation to the risen Christ.

But Jesus was also the center in another sense. He was the center from which the "beginning" and the "end" could be understood. The meaning of history could now be rightly ascertained only from the absolute point of vantage of the resurrected Christ. Paul Tillich brilliantly illustrated this point when he wrote: "In the case of spatial measurements the beginning and the end of a track determine the location of its middle point; but in the case of history in the true sense the historical point which reveals the meaning of the whole process must be called the center, because it alone gives a meaning to 'beginning' and 'end.' And for Christian faith that point is Christ."[4]

For the Apostle Paul, the resurrected Christ gave meaning and value to all that had gone before and all that would come afterwards. The resurrection event carried with it a unique meaning which the Holy Spirit would not allow Paul to forget or neglect. "Paul's gospel," Wolfhart Pannenberg says succinctly, "is the exegesis of the appearance of the resurrected Jesus that he experienced."[5]

THE MEANING OF JESUS FOR THE PAST

What significance did Jesus' resurrection have for Paul and his Christian contemporaries who shared the apocalyptic vision of Judaism? What precisely was its meaning for their shared past?

The immediate significance of Jesus' resurrection was

that it confirmed Jesus' divinity as nothing else could. Claims to divinity were strongly intimated before the Resurrection. Jesus taught with the authority of God. He performed miraculous works. He forgave sin. He accepted Peter's confession of Him as Messiah and Son of God. He applied the "Son of Man" title to Himself, which in Judaism represented the eschatological Messiah. But none of these confirmed Jesus' divinity as did His resurrection from the dead. Old Testament prophetic sayings depended upon their fulfillment to insure their truthfulness (Deuteronomy 18:15-22). Jesus' resurrection was the fulfillment of all prior claims to His divine person. He asked for no other truth standard than that to which the Jews were accustomed. The Jewish way of verifying prophetic statement was historical event. What happens is true. What does not happen is not true. It was as simple as that.

In Judaism there was no place for empty assertions. Historical event was the only means of confirming the Word. And conversely, the Word was the means of interpreting the event. What Jesus proclaimed to His disciples prior to the Resurrection provided the basis for understanding the Resurrection event. Together, Word and event provided the basis for Christian faith. Jesus' resurrection was the connecting link between spoken claims and divine confirmation of Jesus' divine nature.

Jesus' resurrection meant then that God's approval was on Jesus' death and resurrection. He had been "put to death for our trespasses and raised for our justification." Those who believed in Him would be fully justified before God (Romans 4:25; 1 Timothy 3:16). The resurrection verified the divinity of Christ and served as the church's proclamation of Jesus as Savior and Lord. "Let all Israel be assured of this," Peter said on the Day of Pentecost, "God has made this Jesus, whom you crucified, both Lord and Christ" (Acts 2:36 with similar speeches in Acts 3:15; 5:30 ff.)

Convinced in heart and mind that Jesus of Nazareth was God incarnate, the church then knew Jesus Christ to be the frame of reference for understanding the past. The present and the future could now be meaningfully connected with God's purpose from the begining. God's saving purpose could now be seen in the light of the resurrected Christ. The divine logic of the Redeemer God is the Creator God who creates in order to complete His saving purpose. Paul saw the connection clearly and wrote of it in his letter to the church at Ephesus:

> "Blessed be the God and Father of our Lord Jesus Christ, who has blessed us in Christ with every spiritual blessing in the heavenly places, even as he chose us in him before the foundation of the world, that we should be holy and blameless before him. He destined us in love to be his sons through Jesus Christ, according to the purpose of his will, to the praise of his glorious grace which he freely bestowed on us in the Beloved. In him we have redemption through his blood, the forgiveness of our trespasses, according to the riches of his grace which he lavished upon us. For he has made known to us in all wisdom and insight the mystery of his will, according to his purpose which he set forth in Christ as a plan for the fullness of time, to unite all things in him, things in heaven and things on earth" (Ephesians 1:3-10; *RSV*).

Judaism taught that man and nature are under God's sovereign governance, but the future toward which God's will was moving lacked clarity until after the Resurrection. Post-resurrection faith could unreservedly affirm that Christ and creation are inseparably linked (Colossians 1:15-17; Hebrews 1:1-3). Creation and all that follows from it depend upon the will of the Creator. Divine activity is always in response to divine purpose. In Jesus Christ, divine purpose and divine activity come together in a saving act. What God revealed through this saving act He sealed through the act of resurrection. Mystery surrounds the "how" of God's action but not the fact of it. In one of the great early hymns, Paul wrote: "Great indeed, we confess, is the mystery of our religion: He [Christ] was manifested in the flesh . . . believed on in the world, taken up in glory" (Timothy 3:16; *RSV*).

There is a common care of proclaimed affirmations

about the resurrected Christ in the New Testament which shed a great deal of light on the meaning which Christ had for interpreting the Jewish past. They form a part of what is called the *kerygma* (a Greek word meaning "the proclamation"):

(1) The promises of God made in Old Testament days have now been fulfilled, and the Messiah has come:

(2) He is Jesus of Nazareth, who

    (a) Went about doing good and executing mighty works by the power of God

    (b) Was crucified according to the purpose of God

    (c) Was raised by God from the dead

    (d) Is exalted by God and given the name "Lord;"

    (e) Will come again for judgment and the restoration of all things.

(3) Therefore, all who hear the message should repent and be baptized.[6]

Examination of the *kerygma* confirms what has been said. The Jesus whom the early church proclaimed was understood by post-Resurrection believers to be both the goal and the fulfillment of their Jewish past.

The Fourth Gospel presents us with an even broader understanding of Christ's meaning for the past. John speaks of Christ as the "Logos" (John 1:1; 1 John 1:1; Revelation 19:13). John was writing primarily for a Hellenistic audience which has no expectation of a messiah. But they were familiar with the logos concept from their own cultural background. They too had the concept of a savior *(soter)*. Through the Logos concept, John was saying to the Hellenist that in Jesus Christ God had come to save the Gentile as well as the Jew. Jesus was not only the key to understanding the Jewish past, He was the basis for a genuine Christian universalism. He was the Savior for the whole world (John 3:16).

Where the Christian understanding of the Savior differed most radically from that of the Hellenist was in John's assertion that the "Word [logos] was made [had become] flesh" (John 1:14). God comes to meet us in the incarnate Christ and His work. Christian salvation is not a form of deliverance from the body as many from a Greek background would understand it. In His agape love, God meets us under the conditions of the flesh. He accepts our human conditions without reserve. The Christ of Christianity is the One "born of the Virgin Mary" who "suffered under Pontius Pilate" who "died, was buried, and rose again the third day."

The Christian universalism that we find in John has a biblical rather than a Hellenistic outlook. The work of Christ is related to the biblical doctrine of creation. Mark begins his Gospel with Jesus' first appearance with John the Baptist. Matthew begins by tracing Jesus' genealogy from Adam. But in the Johannine writings Jesus is the preexistent "Word" (that is, the Logos) made flesh who is Himself the agent and purpose of creation. It is no coincidence that the Fourth Gospel begins with the same words as Genesis.

Genesis 1:1 reads: "In the beginning God created the heaven and the earth." John 1:1, 3 reads: "In the beginning was the Word [Christ] . . . All things were made by him." The wisdom of God in creation is Christ (1 Corinthians 1:24). The first article in the Apostle's Creed acknowledges faith in God the Creator. The second article acknowledges faith in Christ the Redeemer. The third article acknowledges faith in the Holy Spirit. The beauty of this early creedal acknowledgment of the Triune God is found in the manner in which it unites the divine purpose. What God wills to do through the Word He accomplishes through the Spirit. The Word (logos) is God's self-communication, the side of God turned toward the world.[7] God reveals and gives of Himself through the Word. Within the Word itself is the power to accomplish God's purpose. "By the word of the Lord the heavens were made" (Psalm 33:6). "He sent forth his word and healed them" (Psalm 107:20). "He sends forth his command to the earth; his word runs swiftly" (Psalm 147:15). The Prophet Isaiah said that His Word never returns empty but always accomplishes what God has purposed (Isaiah 55:10).

What God purposed to accomplish with man, He provided for in creation when He turned himself toward the world. The divine logic of creation is Christ, and the logic of Christ is creation. They belong together. This divine logic is not the logic of men. To the Greek it was offensive; to the Jew it was a stumbling block. But to those who are saved it is the power of God unto salvation. John saw divine wisdom and power in the logos concept (John 1:1). The author of Hebrews saw it in the creation of the world through the Son (Hebrews 1:2). Paul saw it in Christ as the "Image of the invisible God, the first-born of all creation" who created all things and holds all things together (Colossians 1:15-17).

The work of creation and re-creation through Christ is accomplished through the life-giving Spirit. The Holy Spirit is the Life-giver. He effects God's action as the renewing Spirit who moves in the lives of men, just as he moved upon the face of the waters, bringing order and meaning out of chaos (Genesis 1:2).

THE MEANING OF JESUS FOR THE FUTURE

Jesus Christ was indeed the center from which both Jew and Gentile could understand the meaning of God's action in the past. But what significance did Jesus have for the future, and what would be the Spirit's role in keeping the believer open and expectant toward the future?

Jewish Christians would normally associate a resurrection from the dead, and the presence of the Spirit, with the expected signs of the future age. Could it be that Jesus' resurrection and the outpouring of the Spirit meant that the life and power of the Age to Come had broken into the present? It obviously did. The fact that Jesus had been raised from the dead by the power of the Holy Spirit could only mean that the future was now present (Romans 1:4; 8:11). The sign of the future's presence was its new life. The new life of the future had broken into the present through the power of the Holy Spirit. Those who now had the life-giving Spirit that raised Jesus from the dead were living in the power of the Age to Come. That same power and life which they experienced when they believed in Jesus Christ was the power that would raise their mortal bodies from the dead (Romans 8:10, 11).

The resurrection of Jesus meant that the resurrection of believers at the end of the age is a sure and unfading hope. It is now a "living hope." As Peter expressed it: "We have been born anew to a living hope through the resurrection of Jesus Christ from the dead, and to an inheritance which is imperishable, undefiled, and unfading, kept in heaven for you . . . ready to be revealed in the last time" (1 Peter 1:3-5; *RSV*). The writer of Hebrews spoke of those who are already partakers of the Holy Spirit who have "tasted . . . the powers of the age to come" (Hebrews 6:5; *RSV*).

A refugee poet whom I recently read commented on the place that hope has in our lives. He said that, "Hope is the last thing you lose and the first thing you must find to be truly alive." That was true for the early church! How true that is for us today! It was the early believer's newfound hope that brought the New Testament church to life. Paul based this new hope on the power of the Holy Spirit. "May the God of hope fill you with all joy and peace in believing, so that by the power of the Holy Spirit you may abound in hope" (Romans 15:13; *RSV*). We rejoice "in our hope of sharing the glory of God" (Romans 5:2; *RSV*). The believer does not live in fear of the future as those who have no hope, or as those who live by false or illusory hopes (1 Thessalonians 4:13). The believer faces the future with confidence because he has turned himself and his future over to the God who raised Jesus from the dead. The believer's future is as secure as God and His promises. Christian hope "does not disappoint" because it is grounded in God's faithfulness (Romans 5:5). It is a specific trust in what God did in raising Jesus from the dead and what He has promised to do for us through the same Spirit.

The world knows nothing of this kind of hope. The believer can hope when hopes are humanly impossible, just as Abraham was able to believe God against all human odds. It is such a sure hope that it manifests itself in "patient" waiting (Romans 8:25). It can even "rejoice in . . . sufferings" (Romans 5:3; *RSV*) and be "patient in tribulation" (Romans 12:12; *RSV*).

Our sufferings and light afflictions are nothing in comparison with the "glory of God" that is revealed in us (Romans 8:17, 18; 2 Corinthians 4:17; Philippians 3:21; 1 Thessalonians 2:12; 2 Thessalonians 2:14). Through the power of the Spirit the believer has already entered into the glory of the New Age. The future glory of God is "already" present. The present glory is not the believer's final glorification, but it does anticipate it as he moves "from glory to glory" (that is, from one degree of glory to another). This present glory does not exempt the believer from pain and suffering. We know Jesus now in the fellowship of suffering. We shall know Him at last in the power of bodily resurrection and glorification. When Christ returns at the end of the age we shall be changed. This corruptible body will put on incorruption; this mortal nature will put on immortality (1 Corinthians 15:52, 53). John said, "Beloved, we are God's children now; it does not yet appear what we shall be, but we know that when he appears we shall be like him, for we shall see him as he is" (1 John 3:2).

God's claim on our life has already begun. The future hope of glory which the believer is already experiencing causes him to long for the consummation. As Hendrikus Berkhof expressed it, "In the light of what God has given, we discover how much the present situation of our world clashes with God's gifts in Christ and in the Spirit. That makes us look forward eagerly to a world that is re-created according to the gifts already bestowed upon us. In faith and hope we revolt against the status quo. The joy in what we possess evokes the groaning about what we do not yet possess."[8]

Christian hope is not escapist in character. A mere desire to escape from present responsibilities amid the sufferings and struggles of this world stands in contradiction to the fruit of patience, and love, and faithfulness that the Spirit bears. Christian hope ought never to be confused with survivors benefits. God's purpose is not simply to "save the soul" from hell but to redeem the whole of creation from the bondage to decay, "For the creation waits with eager longing for the revealing of the sons of God . . . because the creation itself will be set free from its bondage to decay and obtain the glorious liberty of the children of God" (Romans 8:19, 21). Christian hope is a hope for the whole of creation.

The solidarity which the believer feels with the human family extends to the dead as well as the living. The "communion of saints" always includes the dead in Christ. Nothing, not even death, can separate us from the love of God in Christ Jesus (Romans 8:38). Paul assured the anxious Christians of Thessalonica that when the Lord comes the living will not have any advantage over the dead (1 Thessalonians 4:15). On the other hand, the faithful dead cannot be made perfect without us for the purpose and promise of God pertains to the solidarity of the whole body fitly framed together (Hebrews 11:39, 40; Ephesians 4:16).

The future transformation that is anticipated for the whole of creation is already guaranteed by the indwelling presence of the Holy Spirit that raised Jesus from the dead. In the Greek text, Paul used two words that call attention to the Spirit's present relation to the future inheritance of the saints. Both terms indicate that future inheritance is related to the renewal of the material creation.

The first term is *aparche* which is translated in our English Bible as "firstfruits." In Romans 8:23 Paul speaks of the Holy Spirit as the firstfruits of the Christian's future glory. Paul has in mind, as a background of this term, the Old Testament laws about the firstfruits of crops, cattle, and so on that were to be sacrificed as a token and confession that everything belonged to God. Paul uses the concept, however, in a slightly different way. Firstfruits are not what we offer to God but what God offers to us in Christ. The Holy Spirit is the firstfruits (that is, God's guarantee) of that which will follow in the consummation of redemption when the whole of creation will again be God's. The Holy Spirit is the firstfruits of the harvest to come, the present glory of our coming glorification, a foretaste of the coming Kingdom.

For Paul, there is no separating the future of the creature from that of creation. They are linked together by their common origin, the Creator God. Their common source of corruption and decay was the sinful rebellion of the creature (Adam) against the Creator. Their common source of redemption is Jesus Christ, the Second-man Adam. The Holy Spirit is God's guarantee that both will be fully restored in the consummation. This is part of the promise. Peter says, "According to his promise we wait for new heavens and a new earth in which righteousness dwells" (2 Peter 3:13, *RSV;* see Isaiah 65:17; Revelation 21:1).

Redemption will not be complete without the "redemption of our bodies" (Romans 8:23, *RSV*). Paul did not advocate a liberation from the body, as the gnostics, but a redemption of the body. Our redemption will be complete when our bodies are redeemed. Paul assured the Corinthians that the resurrection would be bodily, an imperishable "spiritual body" (1 Corinthians 15:44, *RSV*). The Holy Spirit will be the agent of the new creature and the new creation that God will bring forth in the end-time, just as He was the agent in the original creation. Believers have not yet experienced all that they will experience in terms of re-creation. But the indwelling Holy Spirit is even now the firstfruits of all that is yet to come.

The second term Paul uses is *arrabon.* This term is borrowed from the business language of the Near East. When a buyer cannot pay the entire price in a transaction, he gives a "pledge" or a "guarantee" as a first installment. This down payment guarantees the intention of the buyer to pay the full amount at a future time. Again, Paul uses this term *arrabon* in regard to the Holy Spirit. The Holy Spirit who indwells us is God's pledge to us that He will bring our redemption to full completion. God will complete the transaction at the promised time (2 Corinthians 1:22; 5:5; Ephesians 1:14). The Holy Spirit is the guarantee of our future inheritance, and He is at the same time an advance installment of it (2

Corinthians 5:5; Ephesians 1:13). He is our guarantee that what God has begun He will finish (Ephesians 1:14; Romans 8:16, 17, 23; Philippians 1:6). Together, *aparche* and *arrabon* enrich our understanding of the Holy Spirit's present relationship to the Christian's hope for the future.

THE MEANING OF JESUS FOR THE PRESENT

Hope is more than future expectations. it is a means of drawing the future into the present. Just as a child prepares to become an adult by accepting disciplines and future roles, so too the Christian anticipates the future through what he becomes in the present.[9] Hope, like faith and love, is expressed through the character of one's life. It is never a matter of human achievement or training. Hope is a gift of the Spirit, but it also contains a task. It is never passive, for hope works now toward being what it fully expects to become in the future. Just as the hopeful heir to immeasurable wealth is lavishly generous even while he is still on a meager allowance, the Christian is generously blessed of God with the gifts of the future even while he presently lives on the earnest of his inheritance. But what he hopes to become transforms what he presently is, for "everyone who has this hope in him purifies himself" (1 John 3:3, *NIV*).

The meaning which the future has for the present is beautifully portrayed in the Fourth Gospel. In his Gospel, John substitutes the motif of "eternal life" for the much emphasized "kingdom of God" message of the synoptics. Eternal life does not simply mean the extension of life after death (though it means that too). It means that a different quality of life has already been introduced by Christ and made available through the Holy Spirit. Eternal life is a present reality. Through the Holy Spirit the Christian is already experiencing the life of the Kingdom.

The new beginning, the "new birth," does not have to await Jesus' second coming (John 3:3). It does not depend upon a cataclysmic change in temporal history as envisioned in Jewish apocalyptic. Like all New Testament writers, John anticipated the personal return of Christ to consummate this present age. But this was not his emphasis. John's emphasis was upon the eternal life that the believer already enjoys through the indwelling Holy Spirit. Those in whom the Spirit dwells already have the life of the New Age. It is a personal reality that does not have to await the end of history. Life is not something that God expects us to endure while we await a transhistorical salvation. Christ has made it possible for believers to have a more abundant life now.

Martin Luther called John 3:16 the "gospel in miniature." The good news of the gospel is that God expressed His redemptive love for us in Jesus Christ. The Spirit of Christ in believers gives them the same love for others that Jesus had for those in the world. But love cannot be an abstract idea. It must be enfleshed. Christians are not transported out of the world, nor called upon to live isolated lives in the world. They are empowered by the Spirit to live in the world without living by the values, loyalties, and standards of the world. Jesus' prayer for His disciples indicates how Christians are to live in the world: "I do not pray that thou shouldst take them out of the world, but that thou shouldst keep them from the evil one. They are not of the world, even as I am not of the world. Sanctify them in the truth; thy word is truth. As thou didst send me into the world, so I have sent them into the world" (John 17:15-18, RSV).

Life in the Spirit meant something victorious for Paul. It meant that the believer already enjoys an eschatological existence. Through the Spirit's appropriation of Christ's salvation deed, the believer stands in grace (Romans 5:2). The eternal life of the future is already present. God's love has been poured into our hearts through the Holy Spirit (Romans 5:5). The "joy" and "peace," which are an eschatological reality that transcend all earthly pleasure, now grace the inner life of the Christian (Romans 2:10; 8:6; 14:17; 15:13). These virtues do not result from anything within the world, but from the Christian's relatedness to the future. In Galatians Paul lists love, joy, peace, patience, kindness, goodness, faithfulness, gentleness, and self-control as fruit borne by the Spirit in the believer's life. The fruit of the Spirit identifies the new existence of the believers as new life according to the Spirit.

Paul reminded the Galatians that they had received the Spirit "through the hearing of faith and not by the works of the law" (Galatians 3:2, 5). The boast of one's own righteousness by the Law is the boast of the flesh and the denial of God's provision in Jesus Christ. The Christian cannot live in his own strength any more than he can live in the strength of others. What God has begun through the Spirit (pneuma) cannot be sustained nor supplanted by the flesh (sarx). Paul asked the Galatians, "Are you so foolish? Having begun with the Spirit, are you now ending with the flesh?" (Galatians 3:3, *RSV*).

The eschatological existence of the believer is again described by Paul in chapter eight of Romans. Those who live according to the Spirit are no longer dominated by the "law of sin and death," the old man Adam. The Spirit of life in Jesus Christ sets us free from the law of sin and death. Those who walk according to the Spirit meet the full requirement of the Law (Romans 8:2-4). Paul understood the whole of the Christian's life in terms of the life-giving Spirit (Romans 3:3-8). The Christian is identified by the fruit which the Spirit bears (Galatians 5:22) and equipped for service by the Spirit's gifts (Romans 12:6-8; 1 Corinthians 12:8-10, 28; 14:6; Ephesians 4:11). Spirituality has no necessary relation to the more spectacular gifts. Paul spoke of such unspectacular gifts as "helping," "teaching," "serving," and "administration" with the same reverence as he did the more spectacular gifts that are mentioned in 1 Corinthians 12:7-11. Christians are spiritual to the extent that they are attuned to and controlled by the Holy Spirit in their everyday lives (Galatians 6:1).

LIVING ACCORDING TO THE SPIRIT

The Holy Spirit is the power in which the Christian presently lives. The Spirit is God's norm for our lives. He is the Spirit of holiness. Paul has a great deal to say about life lived according to the norm of the Spirit as contrasted with life lived according to the flesh. When he speaks of the "flesh," Paul is not speaking disparagingly of our common humanity. There is nothing evil or bad about our physical bodies. We all live under human conditions. What Paul means by "flesh" is life ordered by the norm of the flesh. We are not to live according to the law of sin and death that was introduced into this present age by Adam (Romans 5:12-19; Galatians 4:23, 29; 1 Corinthians 15:44-49). When one lives by the norm of the flesh, he is controlled by the passions and desires of his former life.

Life "according to the Spirit" is life according to the power and norm of the future. As long as we are in this world, we will live in the presence of sin. But the Holy Spirit offers deliverance from the power of sin and death. Sin, suffering, and death will finally be abolished after Christ comes again to complete the work of redemption (1 Corinthians 15:23, 50; Revelation 21:4), but the first installment of the new life of the future which we possess through the Spirit has already begun to shape our attitudes and behavior. The Holy Spirit always opposes sin and carnality. God calls us to holiness and righteousness (1 Corinthians 1:30). He calls us to "cleanse ourselves from every defilement of body and spirit, and make holiness perfect in the fear of God" (2 Corinthians 7:1 *RSV*). Those who are filled with the Spirit must take the same attitude toward the world that the Spirit has by reason of His "holy" nature and witness. Sanctification cannot be dismissed as a sectarian distinctive. It is the will of God for all His people (1 Thessalonians 4:3-7). It is God's norm for us during our earthly pilgrimage (1 Peter 1:15-17)

Sanctification involves separation from sin and separation unto God for service. Paul reminded the Christians at Colossae that they had been raised with Christ in the newness of life. They were therefore exhorted to live according to the power and norm of their new existence, "putting to death that which is earthly; fornication, impurity, passion, evil desire, and covetousness, which is idolatry" (Colossians 3:5). His advice to the Ephesians was similar. "Put off your old nature which belongs to your former manner of life," Paul said, ". . . and be renewed in the spirit of your minds, and put on the new nature, created after the likeness of God in true righteousness and holiness" (Ephesians 4:22-24, *RSV).*

Separation alone, however, is not sanctification. A person can be sanctimonious without being sanctified (that is, "cleansed"). Holiness of life can only be wrought in us by the Sanctifier. The Spirit "makes" believers holy. For this reason they are called "the sanctified" (1 Corinthians 1:2; Acts 20:32; 26:18) or "the saints" (Romans 8:27; 1 Corinthians 6:2; Hebrews 6:10). Sanctification always works from the inside out, never from the outside in.

Christ's atonement is the basis of our sanctification (1 Corinthians 1:2; 6:11; Hebrews 13:12). He is also our example of the sanctified life. When He ate with sinners, Jesus showed us that our primary concern is to love, not to "protect our testimony." Holiness of life is something very positive; its purpose is not to establish our moral superiority over others or enhance our status within our own religious group.

LOVE: THE CHRISTIAN'S LAW OF LIFE

The Spirit does not close us up in ourselves but opens us up toward others. The cross has both a vertical and a horizontal dimension. True spirituality knows an outward as well as an inward and an upward orientation. Its outward orientation is manifested in works motivated by love. Love revealed in Jesus Christ (agape) is put to work in our hearts by the Holy Spirit (Galatians 5:6). Those who have been set right with God through Jesus Christ live by this new ethical norm.

Love is the distinguishing mark of Christian discipleship (John 13: 34, 35). It is the greatest gift the Holy Spirit bestows. Without love, Paul warned, other spiritual gifts profit nothing:

> If I speak the tongues of men and of angels, but have not love, I am a noisy gong or a clanging cymbal. And if I have prophetic powers and under-

stand all mysteries and all knowledge, and if I have all faith, so as to remove mountains, but have not love, I am nothing. If I give away all I have, and if I deliver my body to be burned, but have not love, I gain nothing. (1 Corinthians 13:1-3; *RSV*).

Jesus said that the whole Law is contained in love of God and neighbor (Matthew 22:34-40). Paul described love as the "most excellent" way (1 Corinthians 13). John, the apostle of love, identified the real Christian as one who believes in the incarnate Christ and practices love (1 John 4:1-21).

Beloved, let us love one another; for love is of God, and he who loves is born of God and knows God. He who does not love does not know God; for God is love. In this the love of God was made manifest among us, that God sent his only Son into the world, so that we might live through him. In this is love, not that we loved God but that he loved us and sent his Son to be the expiation for our sins. Beloved, if God so loved us, we also ought to love one another (1 John 4:7-11; *RSV*).

Love is more than sentiment or an emotional state. Agape love manifests itself in self-giving action. Love feeds the hungry, clothes the naked, befriends the friendless, sets the captive free. When the Spirit came upon Jesus, He was moved "to preach good news to the poor . . . proclaim release to the captives and recovering of sight to the blind, to set at liberty those who were oppressed, and to proclaim the acceptable year of the Lord" (Luke 4:8, 19; *RSV*). When Christians live by that same spiritual imperative, they too are moved to self-giving action.

Robert McAfee Brown reminds us in *The Spirit of Protestantism* that human relationships are generally based on merit. A football team solicits the services of an outstanding quarterback, or a baseball club wants the .340 hitter because of his athletic abilities. Or, on need, as when one gets acquainted with the neighbor because he wants to borrow his ladder, or with the garage mechanic because his car needs repairs and he needs a reduced price. Some relationships are based on appeal. The young college student does not admire the beautiful young lady with whom he has just started a conversation because she can hit .340 or because she can fix his carburetor. He is drawn to her because she is attractive and exciting. She has appeal.

God's love for us, however, is not based on our merit, God's need for us, or our appeal. He loves us, as He loved Israel, simply because it is God's nature to love. "It was not because you were more in number than any other people that the Lord set his love upon you and chose you, for you were the fewest of all peoples," Moses told the Israelites, "but it is because . . . the Lord has brought you out with a mighty hand, and redeemed you from the house of bondage, from the hand of Pharaoh king of Egypt" (Deuteronomy 7:7, 8; *RSV*).

Our love toward God and neighbor is never as steadfast, or as purely motivated, as God's love for us. Regeneration is the first act of sanctification. The last act is confirmation in righteousness at the resurrection of the body. Between these two great acts our self-giving inevitably gets mixed with self-interest and self-serving. The gap that exists between what we are and what we ought to be involves us in a permanent *metanoia* (repentance). Our failure to love as we ought constantly reminds us that the Christian life cannot merely be a matter of our own moral striving. The Christian is born and nourished by the Spirit. A Christian grows in grace by the Word, by worship, by the sacraments, and by self-denial.

Our life from God is a gift. It is also a task. The Holy Spirit births us, nourishes us, inspires us, and moves us toward a greater love of God and neighbor. This is Gift-love, the love which comes by grace *(charis)* and is properly known as charity. Through it we are enabled to love what is not naturally lovable. Through it we are enabled to find that end for which we were created.

FACING THE FUTURE IN THE POWER OF THE HOLY SPIRIT

Change and uncertainty characterize the twentieth century. Traditional values and institutions have been challenged in virtually every area of life. Global wars have been fought to preserve democratic values, and the superpowers now strive to avoid nuclear confrontation over ideological differences. Space-age technology puts men and women into space with such ease and regularity that it is hardly news anymore. The microchip now makes possible computers and robots that threaten to rival the human brain and brawn. Behaviorists and psychoanalysts tell us that we are really a set of conditioned reflexes, emotional drives, and subconscious urgings that lie outside the control of reason and will. Developments in art and music stress experimentation, the relativity of values, and a meaningless universe. The marketplace knows both affluence and poverty. Many have much more than they need while masses of people literally starve to death every day. Environmental problems, urban developments, budget deficits, peacekeeping efforts, and other crucial issues face us constantly.

Living in a world that is vastly different from what it was a few years ago, and one that will probably change with accelerated speed in the years to come, we tend to face the future with a greater anxiety and uncertainty than ever before. The twentieth century has been called many things. H. G. Wells described it as the Age of Confusion. W. H. Auden called it an Age of Anxiety, Franz Alexander an Age of Unreason, Arthur Koestler an Age of Longing, Pitirim Sorokin an Age of Crisis, Morton White an Age of Analysis, Karl Mannheim an Age of Reconstruction. Some refer to it as the atomic age, the space age, the century of total war, of the common man. Some call it post-modern, others post-Christian or even post-historic. Whichever label fits best, the fact remains that twentieth century man has lost his spiritual center. He suffers from the vertigo of meaninglessness.

Man has tried to find the center of meaning in art, literature, science, philosophy, work, leisure, a return to nature, and other sources too numerous to mention. But these are the gods that have failed. The spiritual center can only be found through the person and power of the Holy Spirit. He is the One who sets that center in Jesus Christ and then makes possible our relationship to Him. Man's essential problem is not a lack of genius, or a failure of nerve, but a loss of purpose that can be found only through the power of the Holy Spirit.

Christians who are indwelt by the Holy Spirit need not escape to an idyllic past nor live in anxiety or dread about the uncertain future. The Holy Spirit is the eternal Spirit. He knows the future as He knows the past. He is the power of the future who indwells us now. It is the Holy Spirit who keeps us open to the future that God has in store for us. We know that our Lord will soon come to consummate this present age. We do not wait passively or apathetically for it is the Christian conviction that God manifests Himself in all of life. We will faithfully occupy until He comes. The forms through which we express our faith may change, with time; the methods through which we minister to the needs of a dynamic society may alter, with circumstances; but, so long as we are indwelt by the Holy Spirit, the purpose and the power will remain.

FOOTNOTES

[1]For an understanding of ancient man's concept of nature and time see Mircea Eliade's excellent work *Cosmos and History* and Henri Frankfort's *Before Philosophy.*

[2]For an excellent survey of scholarly opinion regarding the meaning of apocalyptic literature and its relation to the New Testament interpretation of hope see French L. Arrington, *Paul's Aeon Theology* in *1 Corinthians* (Washington, D. C.: University Press, 1977), pp. 1-65.

[3]R. Hollis Gause, *Living in the Spirit* (Cleveland, TN.: Pathway Press, 1980), pp. 70, 71.

[4]Paul Tillich, *The Interpretation of History*, p. 32. One also finds this emphasis upon Christ as the key to the meaning of history in such diverse theologians as Barth, Gogarten, C. H. Dodd, and Reinhold Niebuhr.

[5]Wolfhart Pannenberg, *Jesus—God and Man* (Philadelphia: Westminster Press, 1968), p. 73.

[6]Bruce Metzger, *The New Testament: Its Background, Growth, and Content* (New York: Abingdon Press, 1965), p. 177.

[7]For a good understanding of the Christian meaning of the Logos and Incarnation, particularly in relation to Hellenistic thinking, see Anders Nygren *Agape and Eros*, trans. Philip S. Watson (Philadelphia: Westminster Press, 1953), pp. 278, 279; 400-404. See also Part IV of Oscar Cullman's *The Christology of the New Testament.*

[8]Hendrikus Berkhof, *The Doctrine of the Holy Spirit* (Richmond, Va.: Knox, 1964), p. 107

[9]H. Richard Niebuhr, "Reflections on Faith, Hope and Love," *Journal of Religious Ethics 2* (Spring, 1974), pp. 151-156.

"This book may well become the standard, even the classic, resource on the Holy Spirit in our generation. It is a worthy candidate for such a happy possibility."—Charles W. Conn

Power With Purpose is a unique contribution to current Christian literature on the person and work of the Holy Spirit. Writing from a Pentecostal perspective, the author describes the work and purpose of the Holy Spirit as it relates to our daily lives and the historic doctrines of the Christian faith. He provides a historical framework from which the Pentecostal perspective can be compared with that of the Roman Catholic and mainline Protestant views of the Holy Spirit. But above all, he shows us what the Scriptures teach about this vital subject. Here at last is a balanced perspective of the Holy Spirit that will serve the needs of laity and clergy alike.

The author, John A. Sims, is an ordained minister and former pastor in the Church of God. He was educated at Lee College, Roosevelt University, and Florida State University where he earned the Ph.D. in religion and the humanities. In 1977/78 the author served as a visiting lecturer at the European Bible Seminary in Rudersberg, West Germany. In 1981/82 he was invited to Princeton Theological Seminary as a Visiting Fellow, and in 1983 he studied at Harvard University as an NEH Fellow. Dr. Sims is presently serving as Acting Chairman of the Department of Bible and Christian Ministries at Lee College in Cleveland, Tennessee. He and his wife Patricia Kay have three sons, John Patrick, Mark Ivan, and Matthew Ian.